Reinventing Clinical Decision Support

Data Analytics, Artificial Intelligence, and Diagnostic Reasoning

T0384085

Reinventing Clinical Decision Support

Data Analytics, Artificial Intelligence, and Diagnostic Reasoning

Paul Cerrato and **John Halamka**

A PRODUCTIVITY PRESS BOOK

CRC Press
Taylor & Francis Group
6000 Broken Sound Parkway NW, Suite 300
Boca Raton, FL 33487-2742

First issued in paperback 2021

© 2020 by Taylor & Francis Group, LLC
CRC Press is an imprint of Taylor & Francis Group, an Informa business

No claim to original U.S. Government works

Printed on acid-free paper

ISBN-13: 978-0-367-18623-4 (hbk)
ISBN-13: 978-1-03-208185-4 (pbk)

Visit the Taylor & Francis Web site at
http://www.taylorandfrancis.com

and the CRC Press Web site at
http://www.crcpress.com

Trademarks Used in This Publication

Allscripts is trademark of Allscripts Software LLC, Chicago, IL.

Amazon SageMaker is a registered trademark of Amazon Technologies, Seattle, WA.

Apache MxNet is a trademark of Apache MXNet.

CareKit and HealthKit are registered trademarks of Apple, Cupertino, CA.

Carestream Health is a registered trademark of Carestream Health, Inc., Rochester, NY.

Cerner is a registered trademark of Cerner Health, Kansas City, KS.

ClinicalKey, Elsevier, ExpertPath, ImmunoQuery, and StatDX are registered trademarks of Elsevier.

ColonFlag is a trademark of Medial EarlySign, Hod Hasharon, Israel.

Deloitte is trademark of Deliotte, New York, NY.

DreaMed Advisor Pro is a trademark of DreaMed Diabetes Ltd., Petah Tikva, Israel.

DynaMed Plus and EBSCO are registered trademarks of EBSCO Publishing Inc., Birmingham, AL.

Epic is a registered trademark of Epic Systems Corp, Verona, WI.

Google is a registered trademark of Google LLC.

Health Catalyst is a trademark of Health Catalyst Inc., Salt Lake City, UT.

Isabel Healthcare is trademark of Isabel Healthcare Ltd., Haslemere, UK.

KLAS is a registered trademark of KLAS Enterprises, LLC.

LGI Flag is a trademark of Medial EarlySign, Hod Hasharon, Israel.

Livongo is a trademark of Livongo Health Inc., Chicago, IL.

MD-Logic is a registered trademark of MD Logic Coram, NY.

OpenNotes is a trademark of Beth Israel Deaconess Medical Center, Boston, MA.

Optum is a registered trademark of Optum Inc.

Redshift is a registered trademark of Amazon Technologies, Seattle, WA.

UnitedHealthcare is a registered trademark of UnitedHealth Group Incorporated, Minnetonka, MN.

UpToDate is a registered trademark of Wolters Kluwer.

Viscensia is a registered trademark of OBS Medical, Oxfordshire, UK.

VisualDx is a registered trademark of Visual Dx, Rochester, NY.

Wolters Kluwer is a trademark of Wolters Kluwer, South Holland, the Netherlands.

Zio is a trademark of iRhythm Technologies, San Francisco, CA.

Dedication

The first duty of every [writer] is to the truth, whether it's scientific truth, or historical truth or personal truth. If you can't find it within yourself to stand up and tell the truth . . . [y]ou don't deserve [to be a writer].

— Captain Jean Luc Picard*

---

* Retrieved from https://www.youtube.com/watch?v=8AYY5dpzNlU.

Contents

Preface

Reinventing CDS Requires Humility in the Face of Overwhelming Complexity

In our last book, on mobile health,[1] we wrote about the power of words such as cynicism, optimism, and transformation. Another word with powerful connotations is misdiagnosis. To a patient whose condition remains undetected, it is a source of frustration and anger. To a physician or nurse who has become a defendant in a malpractice lawsuit, it can likewise generate frustration and anger as they try to demonstrate that they did everything humanly possible to uncover the source of their patient's symptoms.

The National Academy of Medicine's report *Improving Diagnosis in Health Care* explains: "It is estimated that 5 percent of U.S. adults who seek outpatient care each year experience a diagnostic error. Postmortem examination research spanning decades has shown that diagnostic errors contribute to approximately 10 percent of patient deaths, and medical record reviews suggest that they account for 6 to 17 percent of adverse events in hospitals."[2] An earlier report from the same group, *To Err Is Human,* came to a similar disturbing conclusion. The message between the lines of both reports is straightforward: Medical errors, including misdiagnoses, are often the consequences of being *human.* That same reality also comes across in a recent *New England Journal of Medicine* editorial: "The complexity of medicine now exceeds the capacity of the human mind."[3]

Such complexity fosters humility—or at least it should. It requires humility for clinicians with years of experience successfully diagnosing patients' ills to admit that they may be missing as many disorders as they catch. And the way the healthcare system is currently designed, that is a distinct possibility. When a patient is misdiagnosed by Dr. Jones, he often never goes back to him to say: You made a mistake, please try again. He is just as likely to move on to Dr. Smith in the hope that her diagnostic skills are more finely tuned. Humility is also required of clinicians to admit that the quantity of new research coming out in each specialty each year is so massive that it is virtually impossible for any one person to stay abreast of it. By one estimate, a new medical journal article is published once every 26 seconds, which translates to about 5,000 articles per day.[4]

Many diagnostic aids are now available to help address the epidemic of diagnostic errors we now face. Clinical decision support (CDS) systems, for example, are designed to help practitioners stay up to date on new developments without requiring them to spend their entire day reading the medical literature. Some CDS systems also offer symptom finders, decision trees, and other advanced features. But today's digital tools only scratch the surface. Incorporating newly developed algorithms that take advantage of machine learning, neural networks, and a variety of other types of artificial intelligence (AI) can help address many of the shortcomings of human intelligence.

Fatima Paruk, MD, MPH, the chief medical officer at Allscripts, said it best: "[W]ith machine learning, clinical decision support can do so much more. We can transform systems laden with meaningless alerts to intelligent workflows and best practices driven by relevant patient history . . . Machine learning can enable clinical decision support based on multi-system analysis to understand which patients are at highest risk of a negative outcome, or to optimize treatment in real-time . . . Algorithms can parse available historical and current information to inform clinicians which patients are at risk for specific outcomes or deliver personalized treatment plans for patients with chronic conditions."[5]

When will this next generation of CDS tools be available for clinicians in the trenches? When will we *reinvent* CDS? As the 8 chapters of this book point out, these tools are already emerging. Ignoring their value puts both clinicians and patients at risk.

This book begins with an examination of the diagnostic reasoning process itself, which includes how diagnostic errors are measured, what technological and cognitive errors are to blame, and what solutions are most likely to improve the process. It explores Type 1 and Type 2 reasoning methods, cognitive mistakes such as availability bias, affective bias, and anchoring, and potential solutions such as the Human Diagnosis Project.

AI and machine learning are explored at length, with plain clinical English explanations of convolutional neural networks, back propagation, and digital image analysis. Real-world examples of how these tools are being employed are also discussed, including the landmark Google study that demonstrated the value of deep learning in diagnosing diabetic retinopathy. Machine learning–enabled neural networks are also helping to detect melanoma, breast cancer, cancer metastasis, and colorectal cancer, and to manage severe sepsis. AI is even helping to address the opioid epidemic by reducing the number of pills being prescribed postoperatively. Each of these topics includes detailed references to the peer-reviewed medical literature.

With all the enthusiasm in the healthcare community about the role of AI and machine learning, it was also necessary to outline some of the criticisms, obstacles, and limitations of these new tools. Among the criticisms discussed is the relative lack of hard scientific evidence supporting some of the latest algorithms and the "explainability" dilemma. Most machine learning systems are based on advanced statistics and mind-bending mathematical equations, which have made many clinicians skeptical about their worth. We address the so-called black box problem, along with potential solutions, including educational tutorials that open up the black box.

This book devotes an entire chapter to commercial CDS systems, comparing legacy products to the latest software platforms. The evidence to show that these are having an impact on patient outcomes is mixed—an issue explored in depth in this book. On a more positive note, this chapter explores many of the innovative developments being launched by vendors such as DynaMed (EBSCO), VisualDX, UpToDate Advanced, and Isabel Healthcare.

The chapter on data analytics does a deep dive into new ways to conduct subgroup analysis and how it is forcing healthcare executives to rethink the way they apply the results of large clinical trials to everyday medical practice. This re-evaluation is slowly affecting the way diabetes, heart disease, hypertension, and cancer are treated. The research discussed also suggests that data analytics will impact emergency medicine, medication management, and healthcare costs.

Any attempt to reinvent CDS also needs to tackle the outdated paradigm that still serves as the underpinning for most patient care. This reductionistic mindset insists that most diseases have a single cause. The latest developments in systems biology indicate otherwise and point to an ensemble of interacting contributing causes for most degenerative disorders. The new paradigm, which is being assisted by advances in AI, has spawned a new specialty called network medicine, which is poised to transform patient care at its roots.

Similarly, the current medical model relies too heavily on a population-based approach to medicine. This one-size-fits-all model is being replaced by a precision medicine approach that takes into account a long list of risk factors. And once again, this new paradigm is being supported by new technologies that help clinicians combine a patient's genomic data, including pharmacogenomic test results, with the more traditional markers available in their electronic health record (EHR).

All these new developments would be useless if they could not be implemented in the real world. The final chapter outlines many of the use cases that have been put in place at Beth Israel Deaconess Medical Center (Boston) and elsewhere. These new programs are helping to improve the scheduling of

41 operating rooms, streamline the processing of patient consent forms before surgery, and much more.

Despite all these positive developments, it is important to emphasize that AI and machine learning will not solve all of healthcare's problems. That will require an artful blend of artificial and *human* intelligence, as well as a healthy dose of emotional intelligence.

Finally, our enthusiastic take on digital innovation should not give readers the impression that AI will ever replace a competent physician. That said, there is little doubt that a competent physician who uses all the tools that AI has to offer will soon *replace* the competent physician who ignores these tools.

Paul Cerrato, MA
John Halamka, MD, MS

References

1. Cerrato, P. and Halamka, J. (2019). *The Transformative Power of Mobile Medicine.* Cambridge (MA): Academic Press/Elsevier.
2. Balogh, E., Miller, B. T., and Ball, J. R. (Eds.). (2015). *Improving Diagnosis in Health Care.* Institute of Medicine, National Academies Press.
3. Obermeyer, Z. and Lee, T. H. (2017). Lost in Thought: The Limits of the Human Mind and the Future of Medicine. *New England Journal of Medicine,* vol. 377, pp. 1209–1211.
4. Garba, S., Ahmed, A., Mai, A., Makama, G., and Odigie, V. (2010). Proliferations of Scientific Medical Journals: A Burden or a Blessing. *Oman Medical Journal,* vol. 25, pp. 311–314.
5. Paruk, F. (2018, December 4). HIT Think 4 Keys to Success with AI and Machine Learning. *HealthData Management.* Accessed on December 18, 2018, from https://www.healthdatamanagement.com/opinion/4-keys-to-success-with-ai-and-machine-learning

About the Authors

Paul Cerrato, MA, has more than 30 years of experience working in healthcare as a medical journalist, research analyst, clinician, and educator. He has written extensively on clinical medicine, clinical decision support, electronic health records, protected health information security, and practice management. He has served as the Editor of *InformationWeek Healthcare*, Executive Editor of *Contemporary OB/GYN*, Senior Editor of *RN Magazine*, and contributing writer/editor for the Yale University School of Medicine, the American Academy of Pediatrics, InformationWeek, Medscape, Healthcare Finance News, IMedicalapps.com, and MedpageToday. The Health Information Management Systems Society (HIMSS) has listed Mr. Cerrato as one of the most influential columnists in healthcare IT. He has served as a guest lecturer or faculty member at the Columbia University College of Physicians and Surgeons, Harvard Medical School, and Vermont College. Among his achievements are 6 editorial awards from the American Business Media—often referred to as the Pulitzer Prize of business journalism—and the Gold Award from the American Society of Healthcare Publications Editors for best signed editorial.

John D. Halamka, MD, MS, president of the Mayo Clinic Platform, leads a portfolio of new digital platform businesses focused on transforming health by leveraging artificial intelligence, machine learning, and an ecosystem of partners for the Mayo Clinic. He is chairman of the New England Healthcare Exchange Network Inc. and a practicing emergency medicine physician. Previously, Dr. Halamka was executive director of the Health Technology Exploration Center for Beth Israel Lahey Health in Massachusetts. Previously, he was chief information officer at Beth Israel Deaconess Medical Center for more than 20 years. In addition, he was the International Healthcare Innovation Professor at Harvard Medical School. As the leader for innovation at the $7 billion Beth

Israel Lahey Health, he oversaw digital health relationships with industry, academia, and government worldwide. As a Harvard Medical School professor, he served the George W. Bush administration, the Obama administration, and governments around the world planning their health care information (IT) strategies. In his role at Beth Israel Deaconess Medical Center, Dr. Halamka was responsible for all clinical, financial, administrative, and academic IT.

Chapter 1

Clinical Reasoning and Diagnostic Errors

Although the theme of this book is reinventing clinical decision support, we have not lost sight of the adage about not reinventing the wheel. There is much that can be done to reduce the number of diagnostic errors and to improve clinical decision making that does not require the latest innovations in artificial intelligence (AI), machine learning (ML), and data analytics. With that in mind, Chapter 1 will focus primarily on the basics of clinical reasoning, cognitive errors, and diagnostic errors and what can be done to remedy these errors with currently available technology and human intelligence.

Measuring Diagnostic Errors

Although much attention has been given to patient safety in general in the professional press, relatively little of this attention has focused on one of the most important aspects of patient safety, namely, diagnostic errors. A 2015 report from the National Academy of Medicine points out that about 5% of adult outpatients in the United States experience a diagnostic error annually.[1] The same report found that diagnostic mishaps contribute to about 1 out of 10 patient deaths, cause as much as 17% of hospital adverse effects, and affect approximately 12 million adult outpatients a year, which translates into 1 out of 20 Americans. About half of these errors may be harmful, according to Singh et al.[2]

Among the 850,000 patients who died in US hospitals annually, about 71,400 of these deaths included a major diagnosis that had not been detected.

One reason why it has been difficult to reduce the number of diagnostic errors is that we have yet to find an accurate way to measure the problem—and without accurate metrics, there is no reliable way to determine if potential solutions are having a significant impact. Traditionally, we have relied on several metrics to estimate the incidence of diagnostic mistakes: medical records review, malpractice claims data, insurance claims, autopsies, reviews of diagnostic tests, reviews of medical imaging, clinician surveys, and patient surveys. Each has its strengths and weaknesses, and most are labor intensive.

Postmortem reviews. Autopsies can unearth diagnostic errors by detecting discrepancies with medical records and interviews with clinicians and families. Diagnostic errors that may impact patient outcomes—labeled as Class I errors—have been observed in 10% of autopsies. Class I and II errors, considered major errors, are estimated to occur in 1 out of 4 autopsies.[3] Since autopsies are not randomly performed on the population as a whole but rather in special circumstances, some have suggested that the US Department of Health and Human Services fund more routine postmortem reviews to help the healthcare community obtain a more representative sample of patient deaths.

Medical records. The Harvard Medical Practice Study (1991), which examined more than 30,000 patient records, found diagnostic errors contributed to 17% of all identified adverse effects, while an analysis of Colorado and Utah hospitals (2000) concluded that diagnostic errors caused 6.9% of adverse reactions.[4,5] A more recent investigation in the Netherlands found diagnostic adverse effects accounted for 6.4% of all adverse effects reported in a hospital setting.[6] When the researchers divided these errors into subcategories, they found about 96% had resulted from human failures. The primary causes of diagnostic adverse effects were classified as "knowledge-based failures (physicians did not have sufficient knowledge or applied their knowledge incorrectly) and information transfer failures (physicians did not receive the most current updates about a patient)."

Malpractice claims. An analysis of 25 years of medical malpractice lawsuits gleaned from the National Practitioner Data Bank found that the most common reason for payment of a claim was a diagnostic error (28.6%).[7] The same analysis concluded that such errors were far more likely to be linked to patients dying, when compared to other issues, including surgery, drugs, and treatment options. The Institute of Medicine report also pointed out that about 70% of diagnostic error malpractice claims happened in an outpatient setting, but "inpatient diagnostic error claims were more likely to be associated with patient death."[1] The Doctors Company's review of malpractice claims looked at 10 medical specialties and found that 9% occurred in obstetrics and 61% in pediatrics. The most common disorders represented in malpractice claims included acute MI, cancer, appendicitis, and acute stroke.[8]

Health insurance claims. It is now possible to link insurer databases to federal death registries. These types of correlations have been used to detect potential diagnostic errors as they are related to congestive heart failure, 30-day hospital readmissions, and other expensive complications that are now of keen interest to the US government. One such analysis looked at patients who were admitted to the hospital with stroke who had been previously treated in the ED and released 30 days earlier.[9] More than 12% of the admissions may have been the result of a missed diagnosis, and 1.2% reflected "probable missed diagnoses."

Diagnostic testing. Reports on the frequency of laboratory test errors vary widely, but most agree that the pre- and post-analytic phases of lab testing are the most vulnerable to error. One analysis found 62% of errors occurred during the pre-analytic phase, 15% during the actual testing, and 23% during the post-analytic phase.[10] Test follow-up is also an issue that contributes to diagnostic errors, with failure rates as high as 23% among hospital patients and 16.5% in the ED.[11]

Physician surveys. A survey of nearly 600 physicians found that diagnostic errors were most likely to occur in pulmonary embolism, cancer, drug reactions, stroke, and acute coronary syndrome.[12] An independent survey found that more than a third of physicians had either experienced a diagnostic error themselves or observed one in a family member.[13] It is probably obvious to most readers that surveys are not the most reliable or accurate way to estimate the frequency of diagnostic errors since they are subject to many biases.

Patient surveys. A 1997 survey from the National Patient Safety Foundation found that about 1 out of 6 patients (16.6%) reported a diagnostic error, either happening to themselves or a close friend or relative.[14] A more recent survey found that 23% of survey respondents said they or someone close to them had experienced a medical error, about half were labeled diagnostic mistakes.[15]

As all these metrics have shortcomings and require considerable resources to implement, there has been a growing movement to enlist AI-enhanced tools to supplement or even replace them. Ava Liberman from the Department of Neurology at Albert Einstein College of Medicine and David Newman-Toker from Johns Hopkins have developed an AI system that has the potential to replace these legacy approaches to diagnostic error tracking.[16]

Liberman and Newman-Toker's approach uses well-documented symptom/ disease pairs that have been shown to occur together during diagnostic mishaps. The Symptom-Disease Pair Analysis of Diagnostic Error or SPADE relies on readily available administrative and clinical data from electronic health records (EHRs), billing, and insurance claims to measure the rate at which seemingly benign ED diagnoses are followed up in a short period of time by rehospitalization for a much more serious diagnosis that apparently was missed during the initial patient presentation. For example, dizziness in the ED is sometimes mistakenly attributed to an inner ear infection when in fact its root cause is cerebral ischemia and stroke. As Liberman and Newman-Toker point out: "With untreated TIA [transient ischemic attack] and minor stroke, there is a marked increased short-term risk of major stroke in the subsequent 30 days that tapers off by 90 days. A clinically relevant and statistically significant temporal association between ED discharge for supposedly 'benign' vertigo followed by a stroke diagnosis within 30 days is therefore a biologically plausible marker of diagnostic error. If this missed diagnosis of cerebral ischaemia resulted in a clinically meaningful adverse health outcome (e.g., stroke hospitalisation), this would suggest misdiagnosis-related harm."[16]

In order for a health system to implement the SPADE approach, it must have access to a large data set of patient information that includes 2 specific points in time for each patient: the initial diagnosis and when it was given, and the final diagnosis and its timing. It is also important to have established a "clinically relevant and statistically significant temporal association" between the 2 events. To establish the symptom/disease pairs worth considering as part of a diagnostic error metric, Liberman and Newman-Toker used look-back and look-ahead analyses, that is, they first studied a specific disease and looked back to determine which symptomatic presentations are most likely to be missed. The look forward analysis started with a symptom in the patient population to determine which diseases were most likely missed. Additional symptoms/disease pairs that are credible candidates for this metrics systems include headache and aneurysm, chest pain/myocardial infarction, and fainting/pulmonary embolism.

How large should the data set be for this approach to work? At least 5,000 to 50,000 visits, which would generate about 50 to 100 diagnostic error outcome events. This estimate is based on previous research that found misdiagnosis harm rates of about 0.2% to 2%.

One weak link in the SPADE model is the out-of-network patient. If a significant number of patients with the initial benign diagnosis return to a different health system when they experience the more serious outcome disease, that would skew the results. One study, for instance, suggested that during a 1-year period, 25% of patients crossed over to another unaffiliated treatment facility. Thus, the model is most likely to yield an accurate estimate of diagnostic errors when either the data is drawn from a regional health information exchange or from a health system that has a built-in insurance plan that tracks patients who decide to use facilities outside the one that recorded the index diagnosis.

The SPADE approach is also not well suited to detect diagnostic errors involving many chronic diseases. For example, the emergence of diabetes or hypertension may appear slowly over time, making it difficult to detect a diagnostic error using the symptom/disease pairing discussed above. Similarly, certain disorders with complex presentations may not be easily tracked with SPADE. As Liberman and Newman-Toker point out: "For diseases with a sub-acute time course presenting non-specific symptoms (e.g., tuberculosis and cancer), a more complex analytical approach is required. For example, it might be necessary to bundle symptoms and combine with visit/test–ordering patterns over time (e.g., increased odds of general practitioner visits for new complaints/tests in the 6 months before a cancer diagnosis)."[16]

There may be other ways to measure diagnostic errors besides symptom/disease dyads, including EHR triggers. With the assistance of data mining, it is possible to identify patient records that include clinical findings that suggest the need for diagnostic testing and to track follow-up on these signposts to determine if they have in fact been acted upon by clinicians. A delayed diagnosis is one of the 4 common causes of diagnostic errors, which also includes missed diagnosis, misdiagnosis, that is, incorrectly diagnosed disease, and overdiagnosis.

To demonstrate the value of such EHR triggers, Daniel Murphy with the Michael DeBakey VA Medical Center in Houston, Texas, and his colleagues analyzed nearly 300,000 patient records to look for patient demographics and abnormal clinical findings that would usually warrant a recommendation for follow-up diagnostic testing.[17] The algorithms scanned the data repositories of 2 large integrated health systems for 4 diagnostic clues: abnormal prostate-specific antigen (PSA), positive fecal occult test (FOBT) results, the existence of iron deficiency anemia, and fresh stool or anal blood, called haematochezia.

The algorithm found 1,564 trigger positive patients for these four diagnostic clues. Further analysis concluded that: "Use of all four triggers at the study sites could detect an estimated 1048 instances of delayed or missed follow-up of abnormal findings annually and 47 high-grade cancers." The analysis suggests that many patients fall through the cracks, for a variety of reasons, and setting up a better reminder system to address these gaps would likely reduce the incidence of missed or delayed cancer diagnoses.

Understanding the Multiple Causes of Diagnostic Errors

The need to quantify diagnostic errors is only exceeded by the need to decipher their many causes. The list of contributing causes includes but is not limited to:

- Failure of patients to engage with a provider organization or to partici-pate in the diagnostic process (ignoring patient input regarding signs and symptoms)
- Inadequate collection of relevant patient information
- Inadequate knowledge base among clinicians
- Incorrect interpretation of medical information (e.g., cognitive errors and biases)
- Failure to integrate collected medical information into a plausible diag-nostic hypothesis (e.g., cognitive errors and biases)
- Not properly communicating the diagnosis to patients
- Lab testing errors
- Communication problems between testing facilities and clinicians
- Poorly designed clinical documentation systems, including EHRs
- Inadequate interoperability between providers
- Failure to integrate the diagnostic process into clinicians' normal workflow
- Poor handoff procedures
- Inadequate teamwork
- Fear of speaking up among subordinate clinicians when a diagnostic mis-step is occurring
- Disruptive physical environment, including noise, bad lighting, distrac-tions, poorly located equipment[1]

Given this long, diverse collection of contributing causes, it is naïve to think that any clinical decision support system, no matter how advanced, can possibly resolve all the diagnostic errors that may result from these problems. Many of these issues will respond to AI-enhanced clinical decision support (CDS) solu-tions, but others will require bold policy directives, imaginative public health initiatives, human intelligence, and a healthy dose of empathy on the part of clinicians and administrators. An in-depth discussion of each of these causes is beyond the scope of this book. Instead, we will concentrate most of the dis-cussion on the diagnostic reasoning process and the cognitive errors that can disrupt the process.

Diagnostic Reasoning

Typically, when a patient comes into a clinic or physician's office, they are asked to describe their chief complaint and to fill out a detailed checklist that covers all the major organ systems. That information is then used to guide the clini-cian's choice of additional questions, which usually includes a history of the present illness and a family history. As he or she processes all this information, the clinician begins forming a set of potential causes, a differential diagnosis list. The clinician also brings to bear his/her experience and knowledge, sometimes referred to as "disease scripts," to help form a working hypothesis.

At this early stage in the diagnostic process, the list can be very long or quite short depending on how complex or obvious the patient's presentation is. The clinician will also perform a physical examination, including routine vital signs such as blood pressure, respirations, pulses, body temperature, and weight. Once all these data points are gathered, lab tests, imaging studies, or various invasive procedures may be ordered if the diagnosis has not yet become obvious.

Although these steps are considered standard procedure in most busy practices, many clinicians do not take a step back to "think about the thinking process." And that lack of introspection can open the door to several potential mistakes. Nicola Cooper and John Frain with University, Nottingham, UK, explain: "Even if we had the best knowledge and clinical skills, our reasoning would still be flawed by virtue of the fact that we are human . . . It is not a matter of intelligence or memory—the human brain is wired to miss things that are obvious, see patterns that do not exist, and jump to conclusions. We are also very poor at estimating probability. Clinicians are not exempt from these human characteristics. . . . [P]sychologist James Reason argues that, 'Our propensity for certain types of error is the price we pay for the brain's remarkable ability to think and act intuitively—to sift quickly through the sensory information that constantly bombards us without wasting time trying to work through every situation anew.'"[18] These quick-thinking skills have no doubt saved us from disaster on more than one occasion. After all, imagine if we each had to do a step-by-step analysis of the decision necessary to escape a charging Grizzly bear—obviously not the best time to be introspective. But during a diagnostic process, this fast Type 1 thinking can have its disadvantages and must sometimes be replaced or supplemented by what Daniel Kahneman, The Nobel Laureate, called Type 2 or slowing thinking.[19]

Type 1 and Type 2 Thinking

Type 1 thinking is used by most experienced clinicians because it's an essential part of the pattern recognition process. This intuitive mode employs heuristics and inductive shortcuts to help them arrive at quick conclusions about what's causing a patient's collection of signs and symptoms. It serves them very well when the pattern is consistent with a common disease entity. Recognizing the typical signs and symptoms of an acute myocardial infarction, for example, allows clinicians to quickly take action to address the underlying pathology.

There are hundreds of such disease scripts that physicians and nurses have committed to memory and that immediately come to mind in a busy clinical setting.

Of course, this intuitive approach can be affected by a clinician's impressions of a patient's demeanor, how the patient appeared in the past, the clinician's biases toward "troublesome" patient types, as well as distractions in the work environment. Pat Croskerry, MD, PhD, professor, Department of Emergency Medicine, Faculty of Medicine and Division of Medical Education, Dalhousie University, Halifax, Nova Scotia, Canada, points out: "The system is fast, frugal, requires little effort, and frequently gets the right answer. But occasionally it fails, sometimes catastrophically. Predictably, it misses the patient who presents atypically, or when the pattern is mistaken for something else."[20]

The shortcomings of intuitive thinking were dramatically illustrated in an analysis of over 20,000 patients with acute coronary syndromes. Investigators found that 1,763 did not present with the usual chest pain; in this subgroup, nearly 1 in 4 were not identified as having experienced an acute coronary event (23.4%).[21]

Type 2 reasoning is particularly effective in scenarios in which the patient's presentation follows no obvious disease script, when patients present with an atypical pattern, and when there is no unique pathognomonic signpost to clinch the diagnosis. It usually starts with a hypothesis that is then subjected to analysis with the help of critical thinking, logic, multiple branching, and evidence-based decision trees and rules. This analytic approach also requires an introspective mindset that is sometimes referred to as metacognition, namely, the "ability to step back and reflect on what is going on in a clinical situation."[20] This skill set also lets clinicians run through a list of common cognitive errors that can easily send them in the wrong direction. But because Type 2 reasoning is a much slower process, it is often a challenge to implement, especially in high-stress, high-volume settings. For the slow reflective Type 2 mode to be most effective, it requires a well-rested clinician who is not being distracted, does not have an unreasonable heavy workload, and has had adequate sleep to fully use his or her analytical skills and memory. Too few work environments satisfy these prerequisites.

Combining Cognitive Approaches

Nor are these prerequisites always required to arrive at an accurate diagnosis. In fact, the best clinicians have learned to integrate Type 1 and Type 2 reasoning into their cognitive "toolkit," and to switch back and forth between the 2 as needed. By way of illustration, consider the diagnostic process required to distinguish non–ST segment elevation myocardial infarction (NSTEMI) from other cardiac syndromes. The former is a heart attack that is characterized by a specific abnormality on a patient's EKG tracing, referring to the fact that the reading does not include an elevated ST segment. Typically a myocardial infarction is accompanied by an elevated ST segment on an EKG when there is a complete blockage of one of the coronary arteries that feed the heart muscle; an MI that's accompanied by a non–ST elevation may indicate a partially blocked coronary artery instead.

Suppose Mr. Jones, 59 years old, with a history of hypertension, stroke, and elevated lipid levels arrives in the ED complaining of sudden-onset intense substernal chest pain that radiates to his left leg but does not affect his left arm or jaw.[22] An experienced clinician would likely begin to think intuitively about this patient's diagnosis. Mr. Jones' symptoms suggest coronary ischemia, that is, a loss of blood to the heart tissue. Naturally, the attending physician will want to do a detailed physical examination to look for more clues to help refine the list of differential diagnoses, as well as appropriate lab tests. One finding that stands out in Mr. Jones' lab readings is an elevated troponin I level. Troponin is a muscle protein that can escape from heart tissue that has been damaged by an MI.

During a detailed analysis of this patient's case, J. William Schleifer, MD, with the University of Alabama internal medicine residency program, explains his gradual shift to Type 2 reasoning based on a methodical review of all the incoming data, including a physical finding that's inconsistent with his initial suspicion of a NSTEMI event. That inconsistency is Mr. Jones' radiating left leg pain. One of the hallmarks of a genuine expert diagnostician is their more completely developed disease scripts, and their ability to spot inconsistencies that don't fit into these scripts. That leg pain was one of those clues that might warrant a walk down a different diagnostic path.

Schliefer adds another dimension to the diagnostic reasoning process. He supplements Type 1 and Type 2 reasoning with a third approach: a mental premortem examination. Essentially, he is encouraging clinicians to imagine what would happen once a specific diagnosis is made and acted upon: What are the consequences good and bad? In the case of Mr. Jones, if he is treated with the anticoagulants normally indicated for a typical MI and he actually has another condition such as an aortic dissection, the consequences could prove disastrous. The pre-mortem analysis, plus the fact that the patient has radiating left leg pain, was enough to postpone treating the alleged MI until additional data was collected. Once the patient was admitted to the medical floor, the appearance of a systolic murmur plus chest pain strongly suggested aortic dissection, which is a tear in this major blood vessel; the tear was finally confirmed with a CT angiogram. The imaging study also documented the fact that the dissection extended all the way down Mr. Jones' thoracic descending aorta, which explained the mysterious leg pain.

This patient's diagnostic workup illustrates the value of using both intuitive and analytic reasoning. However, a more in-depth look at the dual-processing model suggests that we need to be more critical of the model itself. Although diagnostic reasoning experts generally take the validity of the Type 1/Type 2 processing approach for granted, much of the evidence supporting the model comes from studies of undergraduate psychology students, and it is based on answers to common sense questions.[23] That scenario is worlds apart from the kinds of questions faced by medical practitioners in everyday clinical practice. And although some thought leaders acknowledge the value of both intuitive and analytic reasoning in medical diagnosis, the general belief is that Type 2 thinking is superior and needs to step in when Type 1 reasoning falls short. This view is not supported by the evidence, which indicates that both cognitive modes have their weaknesses and strengths.

If slow, Type 2 thinking were superior to fast Type 1 thinking, one would expect that experiments in which clinicians were encouraged to slow down and take more time diagnosing patients would always yield positive results. "Sherbino and colleagues showed that correct diagnosis was associated with less time spent on a diagnostic task. Other studies showed that when time was manipulated during the experiment and participants were cautioned to 'be systematic and thorough' or to 'go as fast as you can,' there was no effect on their accuracy. In another study in which the participants were given the opportunity to revise their initial diagnoses, revisions were associated with longer initial processing times and diagnoses that were more likely to be incorrect."[23]

These experiments do not imply that common cognitive errors don't have a negative impact on diagnosis. There is ample evidence to demonstrate that premature closure, confirmation bias, and availability bias do reduce diagnostic accuracy. But some of these errors may in fact be related to both Type 1 and Type 2 thinking. And as Norman et al. explain: "[T]he resolution of errors is not simply a case of exerting additional analytical effort; without sufficient knowledge, additional processing is not likely to be helpful in resolving errors."[23] The operative term is "sufficient knowledge." The research suggests that knowledge deficits are just as important as unrealistic leaps of associative memory in causing diagnostic errors. In other words: "general admonitions to slow down, reflect, or be careful and systematic likely have minimal effect beyond slowing the diagnostic process. By contrast, knowledge deficits are a significant contributor to diagnostic error, and strategies to induce some reorganization of knowledge appear to have small but consistent benefits."[23] The emphasis on a deeper knowledge of specific disease entities is consistent with Schleifer's definition of true expertise, as discussed above, namely: One of the hallmarks of a genuine expert diagnostician is their more completely developed disease scripts, and their ability to spot inconsistencies that don't fit into these scripts.

Finding Solutions

Completely eliminating diagnostic errors is virtually impossible, but there are numerous solutions that can lessen this burden on patients and the healthcare ecosystem. Among the guidelines listed in The Institute of Medicine Report, *Improving Diagnosis in Health Care,* the top recommendation is: "Facilitate More Effective Teamwork in the Diagnostic Process Among Health Care Professionals, Patients, and Their Families."[1] Although there are certainly technological tools that can improve teamwork, at its core is better human communication, and to improve the communication process requires that team members overcome numerous psychosocial impediments.

One of the most dramatic diagnostic errors in recent memory occurred when the first patient with Ebola infection entered the United States and slipped through the cracks. On September 25, 2014, Thomas Eric Duncan was seen in a Texas ED with fever, nausea, severe headache, and other nonspecific signs and symptoms. He told the nurse who took the history about his travel to Africa, but the physician who later evaluated Mr. Duncan was not aware of this travel history. His initial misdiagnosis was sinusitis. Duncan returned on September 28th by ambulance, received the correct diagnosis 2 days later, and died on October 8th. Ironically, the EHR system that was designed to improve patient care may have been partially responsible for the misdiagnosis. The physician who made the mistake said: "[T]ravel information was not easily visible in my standard workflow."[1] This mishap suggests several possible barriers to optimal diagnosis, as stated in the IOM analysis:

- Was documentation in the EHR sufficient to convey this information?
- When is verbal communication of key facts necessary?
- Was the EHR designed appropriately to support the sharing of important information?
- Are the notes in EHRs too hard to locate and share in the typical workflow of a busy emergency department?
- Are notes valued appropriately by members of the care team?
- Does the format of a nursing note (template versus unstructured) influence how key information is communicated?

The other diagnostic problem illustrated by the Ebola incident can be summed up in the adage: If it looks like a duck and quacks like a duck, it probably is a duck. Unfortunately, that mindset can easily miss rare conditions that occasionally occur, when the correct diagnosis is overlooked because most of its features match those of a familiar "animal."

Another issue is alluded to in the above list: "Are notes valued appropriately by members of the care team?" To state the matter more bluntly: Do physicians fully appreciate the input of nurses, or do they sometimes exhibit a paternalistic attitude that dismisses their contributions too quickly? Addressing that issue requires a change in organizational culture and a commitment by senior executives.

Although better collaboration between nurses and physicians will reduce the likelihood of diagnostic errors, including patients in the diagnostic process is just as important; unfortunately, many clinicians expect patients to passively await a diagnosis rather than participate in the process. As we mentioned earlier in this chapter, ignoring patient input regarding signs and symptoms is a serious problem that needs attention. As a society, we should be past the Doctor Knows Best mentality of yesteryear, but there are still pockets of resistance in various regions that cling to this outdated philosophy. We have discussed the importance of patient engagement in several publications, including *Realizing the Promise of Precision Medicine* and *The Transformative Power of Mobile Medicine*.[24,25] In the latter book, we discuss the value of using electronic tools such as Open Notes, which lets patients see the progress notes that clinicians enter into their charts.

Conceptually, getting patients more involved in the diagnostic process may be appealing to many clinicians, but we really need to move beyond conception into action. Several initiatives have done just that. The Agency for Healthcare Research and Quality, for instance, has created a campaign called "Questions are the Answer," which provides concrete steps patients can take to get more involved, including a list of questions to ask before, during, and after a medical appointment; videos that offer advice on how to talk to your clinician; and much more.[26] Similarly, the Society to Improve Diagnosis in Medicine offers "The Patient's Toolkit for Diagnosis," a PDF download that consists of 4 components:

- A fill-in-the-blanks chart to help prepare for a visit, including medical histories, surgeries, major diseases, and procedures, what treatment was provided in the past for these problems, and the effects of the treatment
- My symptoms/pain chart that includes a human body graphic that lets patients pinpoint exact locations
- A medication/nutritional supplement/herbal chart, which includes dosages, how long the patient has been taking the medication, who prescribed it, and perceived effects
- Advice on the post visit[27]

Although much of the above information will likely be asked of the patient when he or she comes into the office for the first visit, it is the rare individual who has all the information memorized. It makes more sense to gather the data beforehand.

Improving Clinicians' Diagnostic Skills

There is little doubt that diagnostic errors have a significant impact on patient safety. When clinicians attending grand rounds at facilities around the United States were surveyed on the issue, 583 diagnostic errors at 22 institutions were reported.[28] Among the 583 errors, 28% were considered major and 41% moderate. Pulmonary embolism was the most common missed or delayed condition, tied for first place with drug reactions or overdose (4.5%). Lung cancer came in as second on the list, followed by colorectal cancer, breast cancer, and stroke. The mistakes were most likely to occur at specific stages of the diagnostic process, with a failure to order, report, and follow up on lab results topping the list. In second place were clinician assessment mistakes, errors during history taking, doing the physical exam, and referral or consultation errors and delays.

Inadequate training during residency is one reason for these disappointing results. For instance, among the 22 Internal Medicine Milestones of the Accreditation Council for Graduate Medical Education and American Board of Internal Medicine, only two directly include diagnostic reasoning skills.[29] Instead, physicians in training are being encouraged to "test first, and think later." Such sloppy thinking has been coupled with staff shift patterns and work-hour regulations that make it near impossible at times for residents to follow up on individual patients to learn if their initial diagnostic reasoning was correct. Fortunately, there are ways to remedy the problem and Massachusetts General Hospital is among those innovative organizations leading the charge.

At MGH, there are early morning intake conferences at which hospital admissions are reviewed by residents from the overnight shift, with an emphasis on the diagnostic process that had been employed. There is also a clinical decision-making course that concentrates students' attention on the diagnostic process. The program includes: "sessions on the strengths and limitations of evidence-based medicine; diagnostic tests (including Bayes theorem, test–treatment thresholds, and serial vs. simultaneous testing strategies); diagnostic errors (including heuristics, cognitive biases, and debiasing strategies); individualization of decision making (including prediction rules and precision medicine); management of uncertainty (including risk communication and shared decision making); and the importance of perspective, particularly with regard to tensions between patient and public health perspectives and the physician's role in managing those tensions."[29] Another valuable teaching tool incorporated into the MGH curriculum to improve the diagnostic feedback loop: Residents are informed when their patients have been readmitted within 30 days. Too many clinicians never learn about their diagnostic failures and thus cannot learn to correct thinking errors, misinterpretations of diagnostic tests, and a host of other problems.

Although there is no substitute for real-world, "in-the-trenches" training to help medical students, residents, and experienced clinicians sharpen their diagnostic skills, there is also a place for case simulations. One educational tool that stands out is The Human Diagnosis Project. This project is an international initiative that taps the collective knowledge and skills of clinicians, enabling them to collaborate on medical cases and questions. With the help of ML, and the cooperation of several major medical associations, the Human Dx Project "encodes their thought processes and decisions into structured clinical data to map the steps to help any patient." Souvik Chatterjee, MD, from Medstar Washington Hospital Center, and his colleagues recently demonstrated the value of the Human Dx Project by analyzing over 11,000 case simulations that tested the skills of 1,738 US-based practicing physicians, residents, and medical students. The analysis used 3 metrics to assess clinicians' diagnostic reasoning: accuracy, efficiency, and a combined score called Diagnostic Acumen Precision Performance (DAPP) (Figures 1.1 and 1.2). As you might expect, the study found that attending physicians had higher accuracy scores than medical students and residents outperformed interns. Similarly, attending physicians who were affiliated with *US News and World Report*–ranked organizations had better DAPP scorers than non-affiliated physicians. Although these findings may seem obvious, the analysis also confirmed that tools and processes used by the Human Diagnosis Project, including the DAPP score, were a valid way to assess clinicians' diagnostic performance.[30] The findings also support the value of collective intelligence, which can be invaluable when trying to decipher a complex diagnostic puzzle with no obvious solution (Figure 1.3).

Participant Accuracy by Level of Training

Level of Training	Accuracy Comparison With Attending, OR (95% CI)	Adjusted P Value
Attending	1 [Reference]	NA
Resident	1.001 (0.853-1.174)	>.99
Intern	0.720 (0.593-0.875)	<.001
Medical student	0.575 (0.466-0.709)	<.001

Abbreviations: NA, not applicable; OR, odds ratio.

Figure 1.1 Medical students and interns were less accurate in choosing the correct diagnosis on the first try, when compared to residents and attending physicians. (*Source:* Chatterjee, S., Desai, S., Manesh, R., Sun, J., Nundy, S., and Wright, S. M. [2019]. *JAMA Network Open*, vol. 2, no. 1: e187006; http://doi.org/10.1001/jamanetworkopen.2018.7006.[30])

Participant Efficiency and Diagnostic Acumen Precision Performance by Level of Training

Level of Training	Efficiency			Diagnostic Acumen Precision Performance		
	Percentile Score, Mean (SE)	Comparison With Attending, Mean (SE)	Adjusted P Value	Percentile Score, Mean (SE)	Comparison With Attending, Mean (SE)	Adjusted P Value
Attending	71.9 (1.2)	NA	NA	74.4 (1.0)	NA	NA
Resident	67.0 (0.7)	−4.8 (1.2)	<.001	71.8 (0.6)	−2.6 (1.0)	.05
Intern	66.9 (1.0)	−5.0 (1.4)	.001	70.8 (0.9)	−3.6 (1.2)	.01
Student	66.5 (1.2)	−5.4 (1.5)	.003	67.7 (1.1)	−6.7 (1.3)	<.001

Abbreviation: NA, not applicable.

Figure 1.2 Not only where practicing physicians able to reach the correct diagnosis with less information, they also had higher DAPP scores. (Source: Chatterjee, S., Desai, S., Manesh, R., Sun, J., Nundy, S., and Wright, S. M. [2019]. JAMA Network Open, vol. 2, no. 1: e187006; http://doi.org/10.1001/jamanetworkopen.2018.7006.[30])

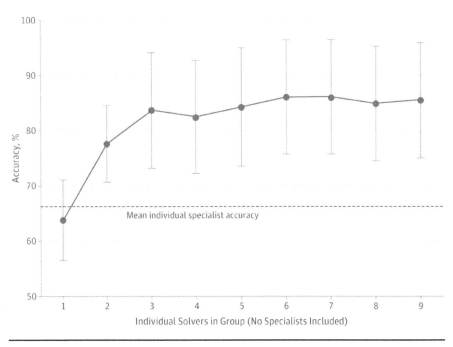

Figure 1.3   Groups of non-specialist physicians were more accurate in arriving at the correct diagnosis than individual specialists. (*Source:* Barrett, M. L., Boddupalli, D., Nundy, S., and Bates, D. W. [2019]. "Comparative Accuracy of Diagnosis by Collective Intelligence of Multiple Physicians vs. Individual Physicians." *JAMA Network Open*, vol. 2, no. 3: e190096; http://doi.org/10.1001/jamanetworkopen.2019.0096.[31])

The benefits of collective intelligence were also supported by an independent study of the Human Diagnosis Project. Michael Barrett, MD, MS, with the Harvard T.H. Chan School of Public Health, and his colleagues analyzed over 1,500 clinical cases submitted to the Human Diagnosis Project that were solved by more than 2,000 clinicians and medical students, comparing the diagnostic accuracy of individual practitioners to that of groups of up to 9 practitioners. Diagnostic accuracy reached 85.6% among the groups of 9, compared to 62.5% for individuals.[31]

No discussion of improving diagnostic reasoning would be complete without a review of common cognitive errors, including anchoring, affective bias, availability bias, and premature closure.[32] During *anchoring*, a diagnostician will get fixated on initial findings and stay anchored to this line of reasoning even when contrary evidence suggests it's best to change direction. The culture of modern medicine gravitates toward this mindset because it encourages physician overconfidence in their own skill set, and because physicians, like many other leaders, believe the appearance of certainty is the best course of action.

Clinicians, like the rest of society, can be swayed by their positive and negative emotional reactions to patients, the so-called *affective* bias. *Availability* bias is common among clinicians who see the same disorder over and over within a short time frame or who have done research on a specific disorder, and *premature* closure occurs when a practitioner is too quick to accept the first plausible explanation for all the presenting signs and symptoms.

Several debiasing strategies have been developed over the decades to combat these cognitive errors, though most of these tools have never been formally labeled as "debiasing." Even the simple act of taking a detailed medical history using a well-documented assessment form gives the diagnostic process structure and discourages snap judgments. So does a thorough physical examination that covers all the organ systems. Similarly, there are many clinical prediction rules that can help clinicians more accurately evaluate a patient's condition and shift the diagnostic process from the subjective to the objective end of the continuum. The CHADS2 score, for example, collects patient data to help clinicians diagnose the risk of stroke with atrial fibrillation; the APGAR score lets clinicians evaluate the health status of a newborn. They join diagnostic and assessment rules such as the Pneumonia Severity Index (PSI) and the Wells criteria for pulmonary embolism, which helps facilitate a diagnosis by assigning a numeric probability to the existence of a suspected disorder.

Other debiasing tools that have proven effective over the years include checklists and well-documented "red flags" that are taught to physicians in training. These signposts force clinicians to take a different direction during their patient evaluation. For example, lower back pain typically indicates some sort of musculoskeletal disorder but may signal the presence of a spinal abscess if accompanied by fever and track marks or a history of IV drug use.[33]

Listening More, Talking Less

Affective bias is among the cognitive errors in our aforementioned list of errors. It can be prompted by negative attitudes about the patient in front of you, the influence of years of societal prejudices, and a medical culture that gives physicians permission to interrupt a patient who is taking a long time to explain their problem or seems to be off topic. By one estimate, approximately 80% of diagnoses an be correctly made based on a patient's history, which is why William Osler's maxim still rings true today: "Listen to your patient, he is telling you the diagnosis."[34]

Listening is not the easiest skill to learn, but one personality trait that can help clinicians develop the skill is empathy. A guidebook published by the Health Research and Educational Trust (HRET) and the Society to Improve

Diagnosis in Medicine (SIDM) includes empathy as one of the key drivers that will reduce diagnostic errors.[35] It is also a trait that can be learned, according to Helen Riess, MD, Director, Empathy and Relational Science Program, Massachusetts General Hospital. Her research and that of others suggest that being more empathetic during patient encounters may in fact have a positive impact on healthcare outcomes.

A systematic review and meta-analysis of randomized controlled trials that focused on a doctor–patient relationship that was built on empathy, rapport, and other interpersonal skills had a small but statistically significant effect on clinical outcomes.[36] The 13 trials included in the analysis measured variables such as pain, weight loss, blood pressure, smoking quit rate, and health-related quality of life. Although the overall effect size—d = .23 to .66—was small, those statistics need to be put into perspective. The effect size of aspirin to reduce the risk of myocardial infarction over 5 years is only .08, and the effect size for quitting smoking on male mortality over 8 years is .08.

An independent retrospective study of more than 20,000 Italian patients with Type 1 or Type 2 diabetes found that those cared for by physicians with high empathy scores fared much better than those with moderate and low scores. The rate of acute metabolic complications was 4.0/1,000 among patients of the most empathetic physicians, compared to 7.1 and 6.5 among less empathetic physicians.[37]

One troubling trend observed among researchers who study empathy is the fact that as medical students move past their first 2 years of didactic training to clinic-based training in year 3, they become less empathetic.[38] Although there are several possible reasons for this attitude shift, the observation suggests that physicians would benefit from a refresher course on empathy. Helen Riess has devoted much of her professional life to addressing this deficit and has developed educational initiatives to address it. The umbrella organization, called Empathetics, includes live training and a mobile app.

The HRET/SIDM guidebook, which the group refers to as a "Diagnostic Error Change Package," includes several other tactics in addition to empathy training, including advice to:

- Provide team leadership training, including TeamSTEPPS and CUSP
- Training the staff on team communication skills, and
- "Improve processes to support team-based debate on diagnosis (e.g., Red Team/Blue Team)
- Encourage use of diagnostic timeouts by all team members
- Engage in shared decision making about goals related to diagnosis and care
- Teach patients and families the importance of accuracy and thoroughness when giving health history and physical information."[35]

It is difficult to overestimate the importance of better clinician/patient communication in reducing diagnostic errors. It impacts the diagnostic process on so many levels. The need for better communication is especially acute in the minds of patients who have had considerable experience interacting with the healthcare system.[39] That realization recently came to light with the introduction of a nonprofit organization called The Empowered Patient Coalition, the goal of which is to promote patient advocacy and patient safety. An analysis of comments from patients who complained of diagnostic delays, misdiagnosis, diagnostic tests that were never ordered, and misplaced test results generated 184 relevant accounts from patients and their family members.

Ninety-two accounts reported patients or family members being ignored or dismissed by clinicians when they brought up worrisome symptoms, changes in patient status, or a failure to improve, all of which resulted in a diagnostic error. Others reported several instances of disrespectful behavior from clinicians, including "belittling, mocking, and behaving rudely to the patient and stereotyping patients. A number of these reports centered on insensitive or impolite use of language. In one especially egregious case reported by a family member, a patient who had experienced abdominal pain over three years was humiliated by a clinician: One physician even had the audacity to 'listen' to her chest with his stethoscope and NOT put the ear pieces in his ears. . . ." Other accounts included clinicians stereotyping or labeling patients, accusing them of drug-seeking behavior or asserting that their pain was caused by a mental health problem.

Some of these patient complaints may have been unjustified and may have resulted from their own prejudices about physicians and nurses. In some cases, it's possible the patients didn't fully appreciate the time restraints that their practitioner had to deal with. And others may have refused to accept that their doctor rejected their concerns because he or she had a deeper understanding of the patient's condition. That said, it would be naïve to imagine that all these accounts are fabrications, especially in light of the fact that the published analysis revealed consistent behavioral patterns on the part of clinicians, and in view of the fact that similar behavioral patterns have been well documented among clinicians dealing with other clinicians. Traber David Giardina and his colleagues conclude their *Health Affairs* analysis by saying:

> *Health systems should proactively develop and implement formal programs to collect patients' experiences, including interpersonal and clinician behavioral issues. These programs could facilitate more equitable relationships between clinicians and patients and positive patient-centered communication behaviors that engage patients, families, and caregivers in the diagnostic process and help prevent diagnostic harm.*[39]

In Clinical Decision Support, Practical Beats Sexy

No doubt, the types of patient complaints documented in the *Health Affairs* study lead to many malpractice lawsuits. And improving communication between clinicians and patients will certainly help address these concerns. But there are other solutions to the diagnostic error epidemic that require attention as well. These fixes may not have the "sex appeal" associated with neural network–enabled disease diagnosis, but they nevertheless can have a real impact on patient care.

Earlier in this chapter, we included communication problems between testing facilities and clinicians as one of the root causes of diagnostic errors. The same disconnect frequently occurs between specialists and primary care clinicians. A report from the Institute for Health Improvement and CRICO, the risk management foundation of the Harvard Medical Institutions, points out that there are over 100 million outpatient referrals to specialists annually, but up to *half* of these referrals are never completed. A single missed referral can easily lead to a delayed diagnosis and a malpractice claim. The report explains: "Of malpractice claims related to missed or delayed diagnosis in the ambulatory setting, almost half involve failure to follow up, many of which involve problems with specialist referrals."[40]

Luke Sato, MD, Chief Medical Officer (CMO) at CRICO, explains that the diagnostic errors that lead to malpractice claims fall into 2 broad categories: cognitive errors, as we discussed early in the chapter, and system-based errors. Although diagnostic errors may result from the failure of a physician to order a colonoscopy, for instance, or refer a patient to the appropriate specialist, CRICO has found that errors also result from failing to "close the loop," for example, a fault in the healthcare system that somehow interferes with the referral process. How serious is this problem? Sato points out that although about 70% of primary care physicians say that they include the patient's history and the reason for referring patients to a specialist "always" or "most of the time," fewer than 35% of specialists say they receive this information.[41] In some cases, the technology is unavailable within the EHR to allow clinical or administrative staff to properly close the loop. In other cases, it is available but not well utilized. The IHI/CRICO white paper discusses a long list of communication breakdowns responsible for the problem, but part of the problem is a lack of accountability. In the US healthcare ecosystem, there is no one consistently held responsible for scheduling the process. Equally troubling is the fact that no one is consistently in charge of knowledge management.

AI vendors can help but, unfortunately, in today's competitive business environment, vendors have been concentrating their efforts on the input side of knowledge management. They have made great strides in developing AI systems centered around natural language processing and electronic dictation, for instance, but virtually no digital tools that concentrate on the output side of the equation. We need tools that can comb through each patient's data to identify issues that a provider needs to follow up on to close the referral loop, and to ensure that patients are notified about test result anomalies or the need to reach out to the specialist's office, when that's appropriate. One solution could be an electronic dashboard that informs clinicians, or practice managers, about such issues so that they become aware of the open gaps and can address them. Such tools may not be especially sexy, but they would no doubt save lives.

References

1. National Academies of Sciences, Engineering, and Medicine. (2015). *Improving Diagnosis in Health Care.* Washington (DC): National Academies Press.
2. Singh, H. (2014). "Helping Health Care Organizations to Define Diagnostic Errors as Missed Opportunities in Diagnosis." *Joint Commission Journal on Quality and Patient Safety*, vol. 40, no. 3, pp. 99–101.
3. Shojania, K. G., Burton, E. C., McDonald, K. M., and Goldman, L. (2002). "The Autopsy as an Outcome and Performance Measure." AHRQ Publication No. 03-E002. Rockville (MD): Agency for Healthcare Research and Quality.
4. Leape, L. L., Brennan, T. A., Laird, N., Lawthers, A. G., Localio, A. R., Barnes, B. A., Hebert, L., Newhouse, J. P., Weiler, P. C., and Hiatt, H. (1991). "The Nature of Adverse Events in Hospitalized Patients: Results of the Harvard Medical Practice Study II." *New England Journal of Medicine*, vol. 324, no. 6, pp. 377–384.
5. Thomas, E. J., Studdert, D. M., Burstin, H. R., Orav, E. J., Zeena, T., Williams, E. J., Howard, K. M., Weiler, P. C., and Brennan, T. A. (2000). "Incidence and Types of Adverse Events and Negligent Care in Utah and Colorado." *Medical Care*, vol. 38, no. 3, pp. 261–271.
6. Zwaan, L., de Bruijne, M., Wagner, C., Thijs, A., Smits, M., van der Wal, G., and Timmermans, D. R. (2010). "Patient Record Review of the Incidence, Consequences, and Causes of Diagnostic Adverse Events." *Archives of Internal Medicine*, vol. 170, no. 12, pp. 1015–1021.
7. Tehrani, A., Lee, H., Mathews, S., Shore, A., Makary, M., Pronovost, P., and Newman-Toker, D. (2013). "25-Year Summary of U.S. Malpractice Claims for Diagnostic Errors 1986–2010: An Analysis from the National Practitioner Data Bank." *BMJ Quality and Safety in Health Care*, vol. 22, pp. 672–680.
8. Troxel, D. (2014, April 28). "Input submitted to the Committee on Diagnostic Error in Health Care from The Doctors Company Foundation."
9. Newman-Toker, D. E., Moy, E., Valente, E., Coffey, R., and Hines, A. L. (2014). "Missed Diagnosis of Stroke in the Emergency Department: A Cross-Sectional Analysis of a Large Population Based Sample." *Diagnosis*, vol. 1, no. 2, pp. 155–166.

10. Carraro, P. and Plebani, M. (2007). "Errors in a Stat Laboratory: Types and Frequencies 10 Years Later." *Clinical Chemistry*, vol. 53, no. 7, pp. 1338–1342.

11. Callen, J., Georgiou, A., Li, J., and Westbrook, J. I. (2011). "The Safety Implications of Missed Test Results for Hospitalised Patients: A Systematic Review." *BMJ Quality & Safety in Health Care*, vol. 20, no. 2, pp. 194–199.

12. Schiff, G. D., Hasan, O., Kim, S., Abrams, R., Cosby, K., Lambert, B. L., Elstein, A. S., Hasler, S., Kabongo, M. L., Krosnjar, N., Odwazny, R., Wisniewski, M. F., and McNutt, R. A. (2009). "Diagnostic Error in Medicine: Analysis of 583 Physician-Reported Errors." *Archives of Internal Medicine*, vol. 169, no. 20, pp. 1881–1887.

13. Blendon, R. J., DesRoches, C. M., Brodie, M., Benson, J. M., Rosen, A. B., Schneider, E., Altman, D. E., Zapert, K., Herrmann, M. J., and Steffenson, A. E. (2002). "Views of Practicing Physicians and the Public on Medical Errors." *New England Journal of Medicine*, vol. 347, no. 24, pp. 1933–1940.

14. Golodner, L. (1997). "How the Public Perceives Patient Safety." *Newsletter of the National Patient Safety Foundation*, vol. 1, no. 1, pp. 1–4.

15. Betsy Lehman Center for Patient Safety and Medical Error Reduction. (2014). *The Public's Views on Medical Error in Massachusetts*. Cambridge (MA): Harvard School of Public Health.

16. Liberman, A. L. and Newman-Toker, D. E. (2018). "Symptoms-Disease Pair Analysis of Diagnostic Error (SPADE): A Conceptual Framework and Methodological Approach for Unearthing Misdiagnosis-Related Harms Using Big Data." *BMJ Quality and Safety in Health Care,* vol. 27, pp. 557–566.

17. Murphy, D., Laxmisan, A., Reis, B., Thomas, E. J., Esquivel, A., Forjuoh, S. N., Parikh, R., Khan, M. M., and Singh, H. (2014). "Electronic Health Record-Based Triggers To Detect Potential Delays In Cancer Diagnosis." *BMJ Quality and Safety in Health Care,* vol. 23, pp. 8–16.

18. Cooper, N. and Frain, J. (2017). "Clinical Reasoning: An Overview. "In *ABC of Clinical Reasoning*, edited by Cooper, N. and Frain, J. (pp. 1–5). Wiley Blackwell/ BMJ Books.

19. Kahneman, D. (2011). *Thinking Fast and Slow.* New York: Farrar, Straus and Giroux.

20. Croskerry, P. (2009). "A Universal Model of Diagnostic Reasoning." *Academic Medicine,* vol. 84, pp. 1022–1028.

21. Brieger, D., Eagle, K. A., Goodman, S. G., Steg, P. G., Budaj, A., White, K., and Montalescot G.; GRACE Investigators. (2004). "Acute Coronary Syndromes without Chest Pain, an Underdiagnosed and Undertreated High-Risk Group: Insights from the Global Registry of Acute Coronary Events." *Chest,* vol. 126, pp. 461–469.

22. Schleifer, J. W., Centor, R. M., Heudebert, G. R., Estrada, C. A., and Morris, J. L. (2013). "NSTEMI or Not: A 59-Year-Old Man with Chest Pain and Troponin Elevation." *Journal of General Internal Medicine,* vol. 28, no. 4, pp. 583–590.

23. Norman, G. R., Monteiro, S. D., Sherbino, J., Ilgen, J. S., Schmidt, H. G., and Mamede, S. (2017). "The Causes of Errors in Clinical Reasoning: Cognitive

Biases, Knowledge Deficits, and Dual Process Thinking." *Academic Medicine,* vol. 92, pp. 23–30.

24. Cerrato, P. and Halamka, J. (2018). *Realizing the Promise of Precision Medicine.* Cambridge (MA): Academic Press.

25. Cerrato, P. and Halamka, J. (2019). *The Transformative Power of Mobile Medicine.* Cambridge (MA): Academic Press.

26. Agency for Healthcare Research and Quality. (2018). "Questions Are the Answer." Available at https://www.ahrq.gov/patients-consumers/patient-involvement/ask-your-doctor/index.html

27. Society to Improve Diagnosis in Medicine. "The Patient's Toolkit for Diagnosis." Available at www.improvediagnosis.org/page/PatientToolkit. Retrieved on April 1, 2019.

28. Schiff, G., Hasan, O. M., Kim, S., Abrams, R., Cosby, K. Lambert, B. L., and Elstein, A. S. (2009). "Diagnostic Error in Medicine Analysis of 583 Physician-Reported Errors." *Archives of Internal Medicine,* vol. 169, pp. 1881–1887.

29. Simpkin, A. l., Vyas, S. M., and Armstrong, K. A. (2017). "Diagnostic Reasoning: An Endangered Competency in Internal Medicine Training." *Annals of Internal Medicine,* vol. 167, pp. 507–508.

30. Chatterjee, S., Desai, S., Manesh, R., Sun, J., Nundy, S., and Wright, S. M. (2019). "Assessment of a Simulated Case-Based Measurement of Physician Diagnostic Performance." *JAMA Open,* vol. 2: e187006; http://doi.org/10.1001/jamanetworkopen.2018.7006

31. Barrett, M. L., Boddupalli, D., Nundy, S., and Bates, D. W. (2019). "Comparative Accuracy of Diagnosis by Collective Intelligence of Multiple Physicians vs. Individual Physicians." *JAMA Open,* vol. 2, no. 3: e190096; http://doi.org/10.1001/jamanetworkopen.2019.0096

32. Wachter, R. M. and, Gupta, K. (2018). *Understanding Patient Safety*, Third Edition. New York: McGraw-Hill Education, pp. 106–107.

33. Croskerry, P. (2017). "Metacognition and Cognitive Debiasing." In *ABC of Clinical Reasoning*, edited by Cooper, N. and Frain, J. (pp. 33–38). Wiley Blackwell/BMJ Books.

34. McGee, S. and Frain, J. (2017). "Evidence Based History and Examination." In *ABC of Clinical Reasoning,* edited by Cooper, N. and Frain, J. (p. 6). Wiley Blackwell/BMJ Books.

35. Health Research & Educational Trust. (2018, September). *Improving Diagnosis in Medicine Change Package*. Chicago (IL): Health Research & Educational Trust. Retrieved from http://www.hret-hiin.org/

36. Kelley, J. M., Kraft-Todd, G., Schapira, L., Kossowsky, J., and Riess, H. (2014). "The Influence of the Patient-Clinician Relationship on Healthcare Outcomes: A Systematic Review and Meta-Analysis of Randomized Controlled Trials." *PLoS ONE*, vol. 9, no. 4: e94207; https://doi.org/10.1371/journal.pone.0094207

37. Del Canale, S., Louis, D. Z., Maio, V., Wang, X., Rossi, G., Hojat, M., and Gonnella, J. S. (2012). "The Relationship between Physician Empathy and Disease Complications: An Empirical Study of Primary Care Physicians

and Their Diabetic Patients in Parma, Italy." *Academic Medicine,* vol. 87, pp. 1243–1249.

38. Hojat, M., Verfare, M. J., Maxwell, K., Brainard, G., Herrine, S. K., Isenberg, G. A., Veloski, J., and Gonnella, J. S. (2009). "The Devil Is in the Third Year: A Longitudinal Study of Erosion of Empathy in Medical School." *Academic Medicine,* vol. 84, pp. 1182–1191.

39. Giardina, T. D., Haskell, H., Menon, S., Hallisy, J., Southwick, F. S., Sarkar, U., Royse, K. E., and Singh, H. (2018). "Learning from Patients' Experiences Related to Diagnostic Errors Is Essential for Progress in Patient Safety. *Health Affairs,* vol. 37, pp. 1821–1827.

40. Institute for Health Improvement/National Patient Safety Foundation. (2017). *Closing the Loop: A Guide to Safer Ambulatory Referrals in the EHR Era.* Cambridge (MA): Institute for Healthcare Improvement.

41. Institute for Health Improvement. "More Than 100 Million Specialty Referrals Each Year: What Could Go Wrong?" Retrieved on April 25, 2019, from http://www.ihi.org/resources/PublishingImages/Infographic_Closing_the_Loop_Referral_FULLSize.jpg.

Chapter 2

The Promise of Artificial Intelligence and Machine Learning

"AI is a once-in-a-generation transformative technology. As such, expect its impact to be on the scale of the advent of electricity or the Internet," says Jean-Claude Saghbini, Wolters Kluwer Health.[1]

"Artificial intelligence and machine learning are set to transform healthcare. From front line care delivery, including triage, clinical decision support and patient experience to back-office operations, such as billing and revenue cycle, algorithms and emerging technologies are already proving their value," according to a recent report from Healthcare Information Management Services Society (HIMSS).[1]

Both enthusiastic visions suggest that artificial intelligence (AI) and machine learning (ML) are poised to transform medicine and bring in an era of cost-effective patient care. But these predictions have to be weighed against less optimistic views, including those that suggest AI will disrupt the workforce in healthcare and other industries, causing many to lose their jobs to soulless algorithms and robots.

Israeli historian Yuval Noah Harari, for example, believes that: "For now, most of the skills that demand a combination between the cognitive and manual are beyond AI's reach. Take medicine . . . ; if you compare a doctor with a nurse, it's easier for AI to replace a doctor—who basically just analyzes data for diagnoses and suggests treatments. But replacing a nurse, who injects medications and bandages, is far more difficult. But this will change; we are really at the beginning of AI's full potential."[2]

There are futurists who are far more optimistic, however. They imagine a scenario in which every patient gets the same quality of care afforded presidents in affluent countries or billionaire CEOs at major technology companies. With the assistance of AI, machine learning, and massive databases, they envision a world in which we each have the electronic equivalent of a personal physician who has access to the very latest research, the best medical facilities that specialize in each individual's health problems, access to cutting-edge data sets, predictive analytics, testing options, clinical trials currently enrolling new patients, and much more. For example, Alvin Rajkomar, MD; Jeffrey Dean, MD, of Google; and Isaac Kohane, MD, PhD, of Harvard Medical School, describe a possible future in which:

> *A 49-year-old patient takes a picture of a rash on his shoulder with a smartphone app that recommends an immediate appointment with a dermatologist. His insurance company automatically approves the direct referral, and the app schedules an appointment with an experienced nearby dermatologist in 2 days. This appointment is automatically cross-checked with the patient's personal calendar. The dermatologist performs a biopsy of the lesion, and a pathologist reviews the computer-assisted diagnosis of stage I melanoma, which is then excised by the dermatologist.[3]*

This scenario stands in stark contrast to the current state of affairs that often transpires in today's broken healthcare ecosystem. As Rajkomar et al.[3] point out, in today's ecosystem, this patient is more likely to ignore his skin lesion for far too long; his primary care physician may misdiagnose the melanoma because of its atypical appearance, and the delay may result in a metastatic malignancy that requires systemic chemotherapy.

With such contrasting views, clinicians have to wonder: What precisely will the future look like? Our purpose in Chapter 2 is to explore the strengths and weaknesses of AI and ML and to help clinicians and technologists gain a realistic view of the near future—a future that promises to deliver more cost-effective, more personalized care but also one that faces numerous challenges. We will explore basic terminology and concepts and discuss AI/Ml solutions in a variety of medical specialties. In the next chapter, we will outline the many challenges that stand in the way of the full implementation of these solutions.

Defining Terms, Understanding Concepts

Ask 10 economists if a recession is on the way and chances are you will get 10 different answers. Ask 10 IT experts to define AI and you are likely to get just as many different responses. AI can be described as any computer system that performs functions that are normally performed by humans. Some experts posit that AI refers to software systems that "make decisions which normally require [a] human level of expertise," whereas others believe the term AI should only be applied to a system that can think autonomously.[4] Of course, even the terms "thinking" and "autonomous" can generate fierce debate among technologists. But for clinicians trying to provide the best possible medical and nursing care to patients, these arguments are mostly irrelevant. What they are seeking are digital tools to improve clinical outcomes and reduce healthcare expenditures. Any assistance from computer hardware and software that helps them achieve these goals will come as welcome news, regardless of the terminology.

Machine learning (ML) is another term that continues to confuse clinicians. For our purposes, it is a subset of AI that includes models that do not require programming with rules to perform their functions; they essentially teach themselves by analyzing a very large number of examples. The best ML systems are created using very large data sets. For instance, the ML system that assists dermatologists in diagnosing melanoma, which we discuss later in this chapter, is trained to distinguish between a normal mole and skin cancer, after analyzing more than 100,000 images. ML and human learning each have their unique strengths and weaknesses. For a machine to learn to recognize a common object takes many thousands of viewings; in situations like this, humans have some advantages. A baby only needs to see a few dogs before it can accurately identify a dog it's never seen before. For a computer, it takes thousands of attempts. But on the other hand, ML-generated algorithms can detect subtle differences in the millions of pixels making up a dermatology slide—differences that are often invisible to the human eye.

Neural network is another term that is important for clinicians to understand since it's the basis for the melanoma diagnostic tool mentioned above, as well as several other digital tools. These networks are designed to mimic the functioning of the human nervous system, with its neurons and synapses. In a software system, artificial neurons or nodes are connected to one another, and as each node is excited by data coming from a digital image, for example, that data is then sent to the next node. The excitement transferred from one node to the next is represented by a specific number or weight. In the case of the skin cancer algorithm, the excitement is the result of the network analyzing the millions of pixels in each image. The process is explained in plain English in an entertaining video clip from PBS Nova.[5] A deeper exploration of the principles that serve as a foundation for a convolutional neural network, which serve as the basis for the algorithms being used to interpret retinal scans to help detect diabetic retinopathy, has been posted online by the *Journal of the American Medical Association.*[6]

Figure 2.1 illustrates how neural networks function. Data representing the pixels in an image can be sent through nodes in the first input layer, which is

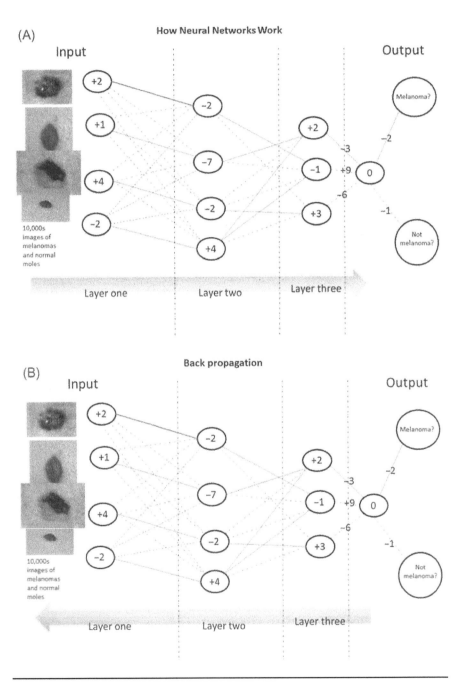

Figure 2.1   (**A**) A neural network designed to distinguish melanoma from a normal mole will scan tens of thousands of images to teach itself how to recognize small differences between normal and abnormal skin growths. (**B**) During the process of differentiating normal from abnormal tissue, a neural network will make many

then transferred to the next layer, with the strength of each signal indicated by specific numerical values. The goal is to arrive at an output— in this case, a conclusion that the image represents either a melanoma or a normal mole. During the initial sweep of each image, the network will make several errors, which are corrected through the process of backpropagation.

One reason that there is so much confusion about AI in healthcare is that descriptions of the technology do not always differentiate between old school and new school AI. For instance, some authors refer to linear and logistic regression as ML, but clearly these traditional statistic tools are not grouped under the term machine learning. Even neural networks can have an old school connotation. But the latest, most sophisticated versions of these networks are referred to under the general term "deep learning."[8] As we discuss in the sections below, these deep learning systems are having a profound impact on medical image analysis, which in turn is affecting specialties such as dermatology, ophthalmology, radiology, pathology, critical care medicine, and gastroenterology.

AI Solutions: Image Analysis

How does all this technology translate into practical diagnostic, prognostic, and therapeutic tools that clinicians can use at the bedside? The journey from proof of concept to evidence-based medicine is a long one. Several of the algorithms and software platforms discussed below have great promise, but not all are ready for clinical implementation. Those with the strongest evidence base fall into the broad category of medical image analysis.

Ophthalmology is among the medical specialties that have seen the most progress in image analysis. Some of the seminal research was conducted by Varun Gulshan, MD, at Google, and associates from several medical schools.[9] Gulshan et al. used a convolutional neural network to analyze more than 128,000 retinal images, looking for evidence of diabetic retinopathy. The algorithm they employed was compared to the diagnostic skills of several board-certified ophthalmologists. Using the area under the receiver operating characteristic (ROC) curve as a metric, and choosing an operating point for high specificity, the algorithm generated a sensitivity of 87.0% and 90.3% for 2 validation data sets and a specificity of 98.1% and 98.5% for detecting referable retinopathy, as defined by a panel of at least 7 ophthalmologists. When ROC—also called area

---

mistakes. Backpropagation looks back at these mistakes to help the program readjust its algorithms and improve its accuracy. (*Source:* Cerrato, P. and Halamka, J. [2019]. *The Transformative Power of Mobile Medicine* [p. 121]. Cambridge [MA]: Elsevier/Academic Press. Reproduced with permission.[7])

under the curve (AUC)—was set for high sensitivity, the algorithm generated a sensitivity rating of 97.5% and 96.1% and a specificity of 93.4% and 93.9%. (MedCalc[10] states: "In a ROC curve the true positive rate (sensitivity) is plotted in function of the false positive rate (100—specificity) for different cut-off points of a parameter. Each point on the ROC curve represents a sensitivity/specificity pair corresponding to a particular decision threshold. The area under the ROC curve [AUC] is a measure of how well a parameter can distinguish between two diagnostic groups [diseased/normal].")

In April 2018, a software system used to perform this type of retinopathy screening became the first AI-based medical device to receive US Food and Drug Administration clearance to "detect greater than a mild level of eye disease diabetic retinopathy in adults who have diabetes."[11] The software, called IDx-DR, is the first medical device approved by the FDA that does not require the services of a specialist to interpret the results, making it a useful tool for healthcare providers who may not normally be involved in eye care. The FDA clearance emphasized the fact that IDx-DR is a screening tool not a diagnostic tool, stating that patients with positive results should be referred to an eye care professional. The algorithm built into the IDx-DR system is intended to be used with the Topcon NW400 retinal camera and a cloud server that contains the software.

IDx-DR is contraindicated in patients who have a history of laser treatment, surgery, or injections in the eye or who have any of the following conditions: persistent vision loss, blurred vision, floaters, previously diagnosed macular edema, severe non-proliferative retinopathy, proliferative retinopathy, radiation retinopathy, or retinal vein occlusion. It is also not intended for pregnant patients because their eye disease often progresses rapidly. Nor should the software system be used in patients who are already experiencing symptoms such as persistent vision loss, blurred vision, or floaters. The agency also points out that the use of IDx-DR is not a substitute for regular complete eye exams for patients with diabetes between ages 40 and 60. However, the fact that about 50% of American patients with diabetes do not have a yearly eye exam by an eye specialist suggests that IDx-DR can have a significant impact on one of the leading causes of blindness.

Unlike many studies that have evaluated AI-based algorithms emerging in healthcare, which are retrospective analyses, the pivotal clinical trial that convinced the FDA to approve IDx-DR was prospective. It was performed by Michael Abramoff, MD, at the University of Iowa Department of Ophthalmology and Visual Sciences, and associates.[12] The study compared the gold standard for detecting retinopathy, the Wisconsin Fundus Photograph Center, to the IDx-DR algorithm and found that "the AI system exceeded all pre-specified superiority endpoints at sensitivity of 87.2% . . . , specificity of 90.7% . . ."

Although Gulshan et al. and Abramoff et al. provide strong support for AI-based screening for diabetic retinopathy, there are still concerns about the clinical effectiveness of this technology. The studies were not interventional, and they have yet to be applied to large diverse patient populations. The true value of deep learning in retinopathy screening will require data that addresses these concerns.

The need for interventional studies to validate AI-based screening was demonstrated by Haotin Lin with Sun Yat-sen University, Guangzhou, China, and his colleagues.[13] They tested an AI platform designed to diagnose childhood cataracts called CC-Cruiser. Previous studies had shown that the platform was very accurate when tested with specific data sets, but when CC-Cruiser was evaluated in a parallel group, randomized controlled trial (RCT), it proved inferior to the diagnostic skills of ophthalmologists. "The accuracies of cataract diagnosis and treatment determination were 87.4% and 70.8%, respectively, for CC-Cruiser, which were significantly lower than 99.1% and 96.7%, respectively, for senior consultants. . . ."

Dermatology has also seen major advances in AI-driven image analysis. Andre Esteva, with the Department of Electrical Engineering, Stanford University, along with colleagues in the Stanford University Department of Dermatology and others, published a landmark study in *Nature* in 2017 demonstrating that a neural network–generated algorithm was as effective in diagnosing skin cancer as human dermatologists.[14] To reach that conclusion, they trained the neural network on a data set containing over 129,000 clinical images and compared the resulting algorithms to the diagnostic performance of 21 board-certified dermatologists, evaluating the ability to differentiate keratinocyte carcinoma from benign seborrheic keratosis and malignant melanoma from benign nevi. The data set was derived from open-access dermatology repositories, the International Skin Imaging Collaboration (ISIC) Dermoscopic Archive, the Edinburgh Dermofit Library, and Stanford Hospital. The researchers used an under the receiver operating characteristic (ROC) curve to make their comparison. A perfect ROC or AUC score of 1 indicates 100% accurate performance. For carcinoma and melanoma, the algorithm generated AUCs of 0.96 and 0.91–0.94, respectively, which were superior to the performance of 21–24 dermatologists.

To confirm the validity of Esteva et al.'s findings, an international team of investigators from Germany, the United States, and France also employed the Google Inception convoluted neural network (CNN) used by Esteva's team. Haenssle et al. used the CNN on an independent set of dermatologic images and compared the algorithms to an international group of dermatologists with diverse experience interpreting dermoscopic images. The 58 clinicians came from 17 countries and ranged in experience from beginner to skilled to expert.[15]

Clinicians were asked to differentiate between melanoma and normal moles and were given 2 scenarios. Level 1 consisted only of dermoscopic images, whereas in Level 2, physicians were given additional clinical details to assist in making their diagnosis. Most clinicians were outperformed in both situations by the CNN. This confirmatory study lends further support to the AI-assisted diagnosis of skin cancer because it was performed with an independent data set and included a much larger and diverse group of physicians.

Titus Brinker, with the National Center for Tumor Diseases, German Cancer Research Center in Heidelberg, Germany, and his associates have also tested the accuracy of a CNN against dermatologists. In their analysis, they recruited 157 clinicians at three levels of experience and found that the algorithm outperformed 136 of the 157 dermatologists. Similar to Esteva et al., they used the ISIC data set for their evaluation.[16] Neither Esteva et al., Haenssle et al., nor Brinker et al. conducted a prospective study.

Machine learning is having an impact on several other branches of oncology, including breast cancer risk prediction. Traditionally, there have been 2 risk models to help clinicians in this area: the Gail model and, more recently, the Tyrer-Cuzick (TC) model. The latter has been incorporated into the Gail model to take into consideration a woman's breast density, which is an important risk factor for breast cancer. The TC model is now considered the clinical standard. However, because assessing a patient's breast density can be subjective, there may be an opportunity to improve the assessment using deep learning to analyze whole mammograms for subtle differences not detectable by the naked eye. Adam Yala from the Department of Electrical Engineering and Computer Science, Massachusetts Institute of Technology, and his colleagues have developed an algorithm that looks at full-field mammography images to assist clinicians in evaluating breast tissue density.[17]

Yala et al.'s retrospective analysis used risk factor information from patients' electronic health records (EHRs) and questionnaires to develop 3 approaches to risk assessment: one used traditional risk factors and logistic regression, a second used a CNN to analyze mammogram images, and a third combined the traditional approach with the deep learning method. They found the CNN model more accurate than the TC model, by a large margin. The hybrid approach was even more accurate than the CNN model. The study concluded: "When our hybrid DL model was compared with breast density, we found that patients with non-dense breasts and model-assessed high risk had 3.9 times the cancer incidence of patients with dense breasts and model-assessed low risk." If these findings can be confirmed with prospective trials, the implications are clinically significant. Nearly 50% of women are told they are at increased risk of breast cancer because they have dense breasts based on traditional risk scoring, and many may develop a false sense of security when told they have non-dense breasts.

Deep learning is also making inroads into the pathology lab, with promising research designed to improve the interpretation of biopsy slides used to diagnose breast cancer nodal metastasis.[18] Yun Liu, PhD, from Google AI Healthcare, and associates applied an algorithm called Lymph Node Assistant (LYNA) to 2 separate data sets of whole slide pathology images. The first set of slides was also reviewed by 1 of 2 pathologists while slides from the second data set were interpreted by 2 pathologists. Comparing LYNA to the skills of a practicing pathologist, investigators found an AUC of 99.3% for nodal metastasis present or absent for the first data set. Pathologists returned an AUC of 96.6% when they were allowed to take as much time as they needed to arrive at a diagnosis. That AUC dropped to 81% when a real-world scenario was put in place: They were only allowed one minute per slide. Liu et al. concluded that: "Artificial intelligence algorithms can exhaustively evaluate every tissue patch on a slide, achieving higher tumor-level sensitivity than, and comparable slide level performance to, pathologists. These techniques may improve the pathologist's productivity and reduce the number of false negatives associated with morphologic detection of tumor cells." In a separate study that used LYNA, David Steiner and associates demonstrated that combining the algorithm with the services of a human pathologist resulted in more accurate detection of micrometastases than either the pathologists on their own or LYNA on its own.[19]

One of the challenges facing pathologists is their lack of consistency in making a cancer diagnosis. The statistics indicate that there is significant inter- and intra-variability. Technologists and clinicians hope that ML-enhanced algorithms will eventually solve this problem by either replacing humans or serving as an essential supplement to pathologists' judgment. An international team of researchers addressed this challenge using a CNN to improve the diagnosis of invasive breast cancer in whole slide images. Invasive disease was defined as the spread of the tumor beyond the breast's milk ducts of lobules.

Angel Cruz-Roa and his colleagues used a ConvNet classifier and validated it with images from three different institutions. They then evaluated it using pathologic and normal cases from the Cancer Genome Atlas and University Hospitals Case Medical Center in Cleveland.[20] When compared to pathologists' findings, the classifier generated a positive predictive value of 71.6% and a negative predictive value of 96.8%. One of the criticisms of ML-based diagnostic tools is that they are too often trained on a single data set and may not be generalizable to the larger patient population. The international team addressed this concern by using 2 different data sets. Comparing the two resulted in highly correlated performance measures (r >/−0.8). Despite these encouraging results, Anant Madabhushi, the Director of the Center of Computational Imaging and Personalized Diagnostics at Case Western University and the senior author of the investigation, offered an important caveat: "The network was really good at identifying the cancers, but it will take time to get up to 20 years of practice and training of a pathologist to identify complex cases and mimics, such as adenosis."[21]

Deep learning algorithms have also been tested to improve the diagnosis of cervical cancer, detect pulmonary nodules in CT scans, and assist in the detection of head trauma in CT scans, all with promising results.[22–24]

Machine Learning Impacts Several Medical Specialties

Gastroenterology. A 2017 commentary in *Gastroenterology*, the official journal of the American Gastroenterological Association (AGA), states: "It is now too conservative to suggest that CADe [computer-assisted detection] and CADx [computer-assisted diagnosis] carry the potential to revolutionize colonoscopy. The AI revolution has already begun."[25] The basis for such evidence-based optimism is centered around active areas of research, including mucosal inspection and polyp detection.

Improving the rate of detection of colonic polyps starts with a metric called the adenoma detection rate (ADR), which refers to the percentage of patients who have one or more adenomas that are identified during a screening colonoscopy. Clinical guidelines recommend an ADR of at least 25% in average risk patients. Tactics to increase that statistic have met with little success, but a computer-assisted system called EM-Automated RT has proven effective by means of 3 mechanisms. The computer system improves the endoscopist's ability to differentiate informative from blurry video frames in real time during the procedure. It helps the physician better detect debris, including residual stool, and, lastly, it improves inspection of the colonic mucosa by dividing the video view into quadrants. A pilot study found that the system produced a "significant increase in the mean mucosal visualization score, the mean debris removal score, the mean bowel distension score, and the mean withdrawal time."[25]

Polyps can sometimes be difficult to detect, especially if they are small or flat, or their color is only slightly different from surrounding tissue. Approximately 22% of all polyps are missed,[26] but a CADe, called a Polyp-Alert system, uses ML–based algorithms to improve the detection of polyp edges, analyzing every 3rd frame in colonoscopy videos. Pu Wang, with the Sichuan Academy of Medical Sciences & Sichuan Provincial People's Hospital, Chengdu, China, and associates, detected 98% of polyps in 61 randomly selected colonoscopies.[27] A subsequent study in which Wang collaborated with researchers at Beth Israel Deaconess Medical Center found the algorithm can detect polyps "in clinical colonoscopies, in real time and with high sensitivity and specificity."[28] This second study relied on prospective data from patients: The validation data sets "were collected after the development of the algorithm and from patients who underwent colonoscopy examinations up to 2 years later."

Although the Wang et al. studies relied on advances in image analysis, there are also technological advances emerging to assist clinicians in identifying patients at risk for colon cancer that rely on other types of AI and ML. One innovative tool has been developed by Medial EarlySign, an Israel-based company that uses readily available clinical parameters to determine a patient's risk of colorectal cancer.[29] ColonFlag has been evaluated in a large-scale study performed on data from Kaiser Permanente Northwest using a patient's age, gender, and complete blood count. The retrospective investigation analyzed more than 17,000 Kaiser Permanente patients, including 900 patients who already had colorectal cancer. The analysis generated a risk score for patients without the malignancy to gauge their likelihood of developing it. The researchers compared ColonFlag's ability to predict the cancer to that derived from looking at low hemoglobin (Hgb) levels. (Hgb declines when colorectal cancer causes gastrointestinal bleeding.). ColonFlag was 34% better at identifying the cancer within a 180- to 360-day period, when compared to low Hgb in patients between 50 and 75 years of age. The algorithms were more sensitive for detecting tumors in the cecum and ascending colon, versus the transverse and sigmoid colon and rectum.

Since that 2017 study, a prospective research project has provided more definitive evidence to support ColonFlag. The ongoing investigation included more than 79,000 patients who had refused colorectal screening. The researchers then applied the ColonFlag algorithms to find those at high risk of the malignancy based on age, gender, and complete blood count. Patients who were flagged as high risk were contacted by phone by their physician and asked if they would make an appointment for a screening colonoscopy. The algorithm identified 688 patients who were at highest risk (87th percentile). Of these, 254 consented to have the procedure by physicians within the Maccabi Health System; 19 Maccabi patients had cancer (7.5%) and an additional 15 patients cared for outside the Maccabi system were found to have the cancer through code matching.[30] Goshen et al. conclude: "The ColonFlag test is a rapid, efficient and inexpensive test that can be applied to scan electronic medical records to identify individuals at high risk of CRC who would otherwise avoid screening."

Cardiology. AI is also finding a role in cardiology. A neural network–based classifier can now identify 10 different arrhythmias in patients wearing a 1-lead mobile EKG monitor, as well as distinguish these abnormalities from a normal sinus rhythm and the background noise caused by interference—a disconnected monitor lead for instance. Awni Hannun, with the Department of Computer Science, Stanford University, and associates accomplished that feat by initially training the neural network on over 53,000 patients and more than 91,000 single-lead ECG readings.[31] The resulting algorithm was then compared to the gold standard diagnoses agreed upon by a consensus panel of cardiologists. The algorithm agreed almost unanimously with the panel's conclusion, with a AUC of 0.97. When the algorithm was compared to the diagnoses of six separate cardiologists, it outperformed them. The EKG data was derived from patients wearing a Zio EKG monitor, an FDA-cleared patch that continuously records from a modified Lead II at 200 Hz.

To put these statistics into context, one needs to consider the computerized EKG interpretation programs already in use. By one estimate, these systems frequently generate errors when analyzing non-sinus rhythms. Among 1,858 12-lead EKG tracings, 254 incorrectly interpreted the results (88% accuracy), but when non-sinus rhythms were analyzed separately, accuracy dropped to 53.5%: sensitivity 72%, specificity 93%, and positive predictive value only 59.3%.[32] If the deep learning algorithms can be validated in clinical trials, they would serve as a major advance in electrocardiology.

Machine learning is infusing new hope into the quest to improve detection rates in familial hypercholesterolemia (FH). FH, a significant cause of premature heart disease and death, affects approximately one in 250 individuals, yet the current detection rate is abysmal: Less than 10% of persons with the disorder in the United States are identified.[33] Juan Banda, with the Center for Biomedical Informatics Research, Stanford University, and his colleagues at other universities have developed a deep learning classifier that is much more likely to find these patients. Considering the fact that a person with this monogenic disorder is *twenty* times more likely to develop atherosclerotic cardiovascular disease than someone with normal LDL levels, it is hard to imagine the algorithm *not* benefiting patients with this disorder—or their at-risk relatives.

The algorithm was tested on 2 separate data sets to address the criticism that these tools are not generalizable. It was evaluated using a random forest design on EHR data from Stanford Health Care patients and on patients from the Geisinger Healthcare System. Positive predictive value was 0.88 with a sensitivity of 0.75 in the Stanford patients and accurately identified 84% of patients at the highest probability threshold. For Geisinger patients, the classifier generated a positive predictive value of 0.85.

Differences in the risk criteria recommended in the current screening guidelines and the risk criteria used to create the deep learning algorithms explain why the ML approach was so much more effective. Currently, clinicians are advised to consider a diagnosis of FH if LDL-cholesterol levels rise above 190 mg/dl and the patient has a family history of early-onset atherosclerotic disease. But in light of the fact that less than 5% of adults with LDL levels above 190 actually have the mutation causing FH, and the fact that an adequate family history is very often lacking, these criteria are not very helpful. The algorithm designed by Banda et al.[33] mined patients' structured and unstructured EHR data to extract a long list of relevant variables, including lab tests, text mention, diagnosis codes, and medication prescriptions. For instance, among the top 20 features were a prescription for atorvastatin, ezetimibe, rosuvastatin, metoprolol, or rosuvastatin; mention of red meat; triglycerides; a visit to a cardiology clinic; the word *high* as a describer for cholesterol value in serum or plasma; very high triglycerides in serum or plasma; "other and unspecified hyperlipidemia"; or "a diagnosis code of paroxysmal supraventricular tachycardia" in structured data.

Endocrinology. Type 1 and Type 2 diabetes have received a great deal of attention from technologists and clinicians interested in improving prediction, detection, and management of the disease. The MD-Logic Artificial Pancreas (MDLAP) System, developed by scientists from Israel, Slovenia, and Germany, has proven to be one of the most robust AI-enabled systems to offer real-time benefits to Type 1 patients. It includes a glucose sensor embedded in a patient's abdomen, an insulin pump, and the software program that connects them. With the assistance of sophisticated algorithms, MD-Logic can automatically handle insulin delivery, taking into account individual variations in each patient's lifestyle, including changes in diet and exercise, which eliminates or reduces the need for patients to measure their blood glucose 6–7 times a day and calculate the amount of carbohydrates they eat during each meal.

The system, which takes advantage of fuzzy logic and adaptive learning algorithms, has been incorporated into a FDA-cleared platform called DreaMed Advisor Pro. The regulatory agency states that "DreaMed Advisor Pro is indicated for use by healthcare professionals when analyzing continuous glucose monitoring (CGM), self-monitoring blood glucose (SMBG), and pump data to generate recommendations for optimizing a patient's insulin pump settings for basal rate, carbohydrate ratio (CR), and correction factor (CF); without considering the full clinical status of a particular patient. DreaMed Advisor Pro does not replace clinical judgment." However, the FDA also required certain restrictions when clearing the software system. It is not intended to send recommendations directly to patients without first being approved by a clinician. In the United States, it is not intended for patients who use an automated closed-loop insulin-dosing system, and is not intended for patients who use insulin formulations other than U-100. It is also not cleared for patients treated with insulin injections or a combination of injections and an insulin pump. Since Advisor Pro analyzes the insulin-dosing history from the insulin pump, it will be blind to insulin delivered by injections and/or IV insulin.[34] A 2013 RCT with a crossover design, published in the *New England Journal of Medicine*, demonstrated that MD-Logic can control nocturnal blood glucose levels in children between 10 and 18 years of age in a diabetes camp. The trial assigned 56 patients with Type 1 disease to either the artificial pancreas system or a sensor-augmented insulin pump. The experiment, which lasted 2 consecutive nights, found that when the children used the MD-Logic system, they experienced significantly fewer episodes of nighttime hypoglycemia and lower median glucose levels (124 mg/dl vs. 140.4 mg/dl).[35]

In 2014, this software was used in a second RCT conducted over a 6-week period. Twenty-four patients were randomly assigned to 2 overnight crossover periods, each including 6 weeks of consecutive nights. Patients on the MD-Logic system experienced less hypoglycemia and more time in the target blood glucose zone than when they were on a sensor-augmented insulin pump.[36]

Livongo is another innovative vendor that is seeing clinical results from implementing AI-enhanced tools in diabetes care. The company combines clinical decision support with patient support that includes customized glucose meters (Figure 2.2) and nurse coaches who send personalized messages to

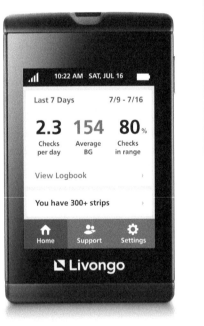

Figure 2.2   Livongo combines clinical decision support with patient support that includes customized glucose meters and nurse coaches who send personalized message to patients in need of advice. (Photos courtesy of Livongo.)

patients in need of advice. The Livongo program uses 4 technologies it refers to as AI+AI, which represents Aggregate, Interpret, Apply, and Iterate. It aggregates data from a variety of sources, including its custom-built devices, as well as a patient's age, gender, zip code, medical claims, and pharmacy claims. The aggregated data is interpreted to create a unique data set it calls Health Signals, which is derived from its applications, devices, coaches, and other sources. It uses these signals to build relevant healthcare messages and outputs for its apps. The Apply in AI+AI refers to the applications linked to its glucose meter, BP cuff, and digital scale, as well as the "human applications," namely, its coaching system and care coordination team. Finally, the system folds the signals it has generated back into the AI engine to make the system smarter.

Several unpublished and published studies support the Livongo approach to patient care. For example, Janelle Downing, PhD, with the Center of Health and Community, University of California, San Francisco, in collaboration with Livongo and Stanford School of Medicine researchers, tested the effects of the Livongo glucose meter. They compared meter users' blood glucose levels one month into the program to 2 and 12 months into it and found an 18.4% drop in the likelihood of having a day with blood glucose readings below 70 mg/dl in the 2- to 12-month group compared to the beginners. Similarly, hyperglycemia, defined as blood glucose above 180 mg/dl, decreased by 16.4%.[37]

Although the management of active disease is essential, there is also a place for AI in predicting diabetes in prediabetic patients. The US Centers for Disease Control and Prevention estimates that about 84 million American adults have prediabetes, which translates into more than 1 out of 3 citizens.[38] Government officials estimate that between 15% and 30% of these prediabetics will develop Type 2 disease within 3 to 5 years without lifestyle changes.[39] A data analysis performed by Allscripts, however, suggests that 80% of at-risk patients will develop active disease.[40] With these troubling statistics in mind, it behooves clinicians and patients alike to consider the value of diabetes prevention programs. The National Diabetes Prevention Program, a partnership of public and private organizations, has several practical tools and resources to address this issue, including a simple risk-analysis questionnaire.[41]

In a previous publication, we discussed the work of Jeremy Sussman, MD, with the University of Michigan, and associates in which they created a data analytics program that identified patients at risk for diabetes. Their analysis found 7 risk factors most likely to predict the development of Type 2 diabetes. Using raw data from the Diabetes Prevention Program, they found the following parameters most relevant: fasting blood sugar, HbA1c, family history of elevated blood glucose, blood triglycerides, waist measurement in centimeters, height, and waist-to-hip ratio.[42]

Several innovative thinkers and doers have also stepped into this space to help identify at-risk patients, including Medial EarlySign, the company behind the MD-Logic software. The company has developed an algorithm that predicts when a patient will develop full-blown disease based on routine lab results, including blood glucose HbA1c, triglyceride levels, alanine amino transferase, white blood count, as well as age, gender, and body mass index. A retrospective study conducted by Medial EarlySign that involved 645,000 patients factored 14 risk parameters into its analysis and found it was able to isolate a subgroup that was prediabetic; in this smaller group, they identified 64% who became diabetic within 12 months.[43]

Emergency/Critical Care Medicine. Worldwide, sepsis is the leading cause of death and the primary cause of death in hospitals. Despite the toll that sepsis takes, its complex etiology continues to confound clinicians; its optimal treatment remains debatable. Several factors have to be taken into account when managing the condition, including controlling the source of the underlying infection, reversing hypovolemia, managing secondary organ failure, as well as administration of IV fluids and vasopressors. Complicating matters further is the fact that there is no agreed-upon way to personalize treatment, which has resulted in a wide variety of therapeutic approaches and poorer clinical outcomes. With these challenges in mind, Matthieu Komorowski with the Department of Surgery and Cancer, Imperial College London, and his associates[44] devised an AI-enabled algorithm to collect a long list of variables likely to affect a patient's course in the hope that it would improve treatment strategies. Using reinforcement learning, the team created an "Artificial Intelligence Clinician" by extracting data from a large data set from two nonoverlapping ICU databases collected from U.S. adults: the Medical Information Mart for Intensive Care version III (MIMIC-III) and eICU Research Institute Database (eRI). With the help of these 2 databases, investigators compiled a list of 48 variables that were likely to influence sepsis management, including demographics, Elixhauser premorbid status, vital signs, lab data, IV fluids given, and vasopressors administered. During their retrospective analysis, the treatment strategies recommended by the AI Clinician were on average more reliable than those chosen by clinicians. Komorowski et al. also state: "In a large validation cohort independent of the training data, mortality was lowest in patients for whom clinicians' actual doses matched the AI decisions. Our model provides individualized and clinically interpretable treatment decisions for sepsis that could improve patient outcomes."[44]

To address the shortcomings of a retrospective analysis, David Shimabukuro, with the Division of Critical Care Medicine, Department of Anesthesia and Perioperative Care, University of California San Francisco, and his colleagues performed a RCT to test the validity of a ML algorithm to improve outcomes of patients with severe sepsis.[45] The algorithm used 6 readily available markers to identify patients most at risk of severe sepsis: blood pressure, heart rate, temperature, respiratory rate, peripheral capillary oxygen (SpO2), and age among patients in two medical surgical ICUs at University of California, San Francisco Medical Center. In the control group (75 patients), the current severe sepsis detector was used while the experimental group (67 patients) took advantage of the ML tool. The subsequent alerts were then used by clinicians to administer treatment. Shimabukuro et al. concluded: "The algorithm uses only six vital signs to provide higher sensitivity and specificity than commonly used sepsis scoring systems."[45]

Although AI may have value in determining the best approach to treating severe sepsis, clinicians prefer to prevent its onset in the first place. Aaron Masino, with the Department of Anesthesiology and Critical Care, Perelman School of Medicine at the University of Pennsylvania, Philadelphia, and his colleagues developed several ML models to help recognize early sepsis in a neonatal ICU using commonly available EHR data.[46] They performed a retrospective case control study of infants younger than 1 year of age who had been admitted to the NICU for 48 hours or longer and compared them to infants with sepsis. Children received the diagnosis of sepsis either because blood cultures confirmed a specific pathogen or because they were clinically positive but culture negative. The team developed 8 ML models based on up to 36 markers taken from routine EHR data. Six of these models were capable of separating culture-positive sepsis from non-sepsis with a mean area under the ROC of 0.8 to 0.82. When culture positive and clinically positive cases were analyzed together, AUC was 0.85 to 0.87. Among the risk factors used to identify at-risk infants: apnea, bradycardia, lethargy, poor perfusion, co-morbidities such as congenital heart disease and ventriculoperitoneal shunt, a central venous line, lab values including bicarbonate and capillary pH, as well as common vital signs such as heart rate, temperature, respiratory rate, and mean arterial blood pressure. The 8 ML models used to develop the early warning system are listed in Figure 2.3. No statistically significant differences were detected among the models.

A similar sepsis prediction was developed by informaticists and emergency medicine specialists from Stanford University and Kaiser Permanente. Their ML system, called InSight, also used commonly available clinical parameters, including vital signs, oxygen saturation, age, and Glasgow Coma Score to predict sepsis in ICU patients 15 years of age and older. Once again, AUC results suggest that the algorithms are superior to commonly used scoring systems.[47]

Earlier in our discussion of sepsis, we mentioned the complex etiology of the disorder. A provocative data analysis from the University of Pittsburgh Medical School suggests that this complexity is due in part to sepsis being not one condition but several.[48] Christopher Seymour, MD, MSc, and his colleagues used ML and AI to separate out 4 distinct phenotypes and found that these 4

Model	CPOnly	CP+Clinical
AdaBoost	**0.83** [0.76, 0.89]	0.85 [0.80, 0.90]
Gradient boosting	0.80 [0.71, 0.91]	**0.87** [0.82, 0.92]
Gaussian process	0.75 [0.67, 0.90]	0.79 [0.69, 0.88]
k-nearest neighbors	0.73 [0.66, 0.87]	0.79 [0.72, 0.83]
Logistic regression	**0.83** [0.76, 0.89]	0.85 [0.80, 0.94]
Naïve Bayes	0.81 [0.69, 0.87]	0.84 [0.79, 0.90]
Random forest	0.82 [0.73, 0.88]	0.86 [0.82, 0.91]
Support vector machine*	0.82 [0.76, 0.88]	0.86 [0.82, 0.91]

*The radial basis function kernel was used for the support vector machine

https://doi.org/10.1371/journal.pone.0212665.t004

Figure 2.3   Area under receiver operating characteristic for CPOnly (controls and culture-positive cases) and CP+- Clinical (controls, culture-positive cases, and clinically positive cases) for each model. Each value is computed as the mean over 10 iterations of cross-validation. Values in brackets indicate performance range over the 10 iterations. Bold text indicates highest performance in each column. The null hypothesis of equal inter-model distributions was rejected by the Friedman rank sum test with p-values of <0.001 for both the CPOnly and CP+Clinical data sets. (*Source:* Masino, A. J., Harris, M. C., Forsyth, D., Ostapenko, S., Srinivasan, L., Bonafide, C. P., Balamuth, F., Schmatz, M., and Grundmeier, R. W. [2019]. "Machine Learning Models for Early Sepsis Recognition in the Neonatal Intensive Care Unit Using Readily Available Electronic Health Record Data." *PLoS ONE*, vol. 14, no. 2: e0212665; https://doi.org/10.1371/journal.pone.0212665.[46])

phenotypes correlated with their clinical outcomes. Seymour et al. conclude: "[S]imulations suggested these phenotypes may help in understanding heterogeneity of treatment effects."[48] Their analysis may have profound implications if they can be confirmed by clinical trials that demonstrate that distinct treatment plans improve outcomes in each of the 4 phenotypes. Equally important, their research provides further evidence that disease is rarely the end result of one cause but rather the culmination of numerous interacting contributing factors. The goal of systems biology and network medicine, the topic of Chapter 7, is to decipher this complex mix. More details on the Seymour et al. study are discussed in that chapter.

Most ML initiatives that attempt to improve sepsis management limit themselves to a relatively narrow collection of demographic and clinical parameters. Health Catalyst, a data analytics company located in Salt Lake City, UT, takes a much broader approach. This company has developed a digital tool it calls the Data Operating System (DOS), which combines the features of data warehouses, clinical data repositories, and health information exchanges to form a single technology platform. As Figure 2.4 illustrates, DOS includes several key attributes that allow health systems to do a much deeper dive into its at-risk patient populations and resurface with actionable insights. The features include registries, value sets, data logic, open APIs, streaming data, integration of structured and unstructured data, EHR integration, microservices architecture, a variety of ML models, and an agnostic data lake. Although the intricacies of how DOS works are beyond the scope of this book, its real-world results are worth discussing.

When Mission Health, a healthcare system in Asheville, NC, wanted to improve its ability to detect sepsis early on in its development, it used Health Catalyst's DOS platform (Figure 2.4A), including its Sepsis Prevention Analytics Application (Figure 2.4B). Health Catalyst explains: "The analytics application is designed for clinicians, medical directors, operational directors, and clinical program guidance teams in the emergency, intensive care, and inpatient units. It provides near real-time actionable data to help improve early recognition of sepsis, early intervention for severe sepsis, and early therapy for septic shock, to reduce mortality. Using the data within the analytics application, the committee can monitor performance on an individual patient, clinician, unit, and hospital level, enabling ongoing feedback on sepsis-alert activations and bundled compliance, including how patient outcomes such as mortality and LOS rates are impacted."[49] Mission Health experienced a 14.4% relative drop in length of stay among inpatients who had severe sepsis and septic shock for patients who had the complication NPOA, that is, not present on arrival. There was also a 45.3% relative reduction in severe sepsis and septic shock NPOA mortality rate.

The prompt detection of intracranial hemorrhage (ICH) is another area in which ML holds promise. Since nearly 50% of all deaths resulting from ICH take place within the first 24 hours, the sooner the complication can be diagnosed the greater the chance of administering appropriate therapy. A delay in performing and interpreting a head CT scan is especially problematic in an outpatient setting, in which a family physician who suspects ICH may order a non-emergent, routine head CT. To address this concern, radiologists at Geisinger Healthcare in Pennsylvania developed a ML-based algorithm using over 46,000 head CTs and about 2 million images collected from several facilities in the Geisinger healthcare system.[50]

Geisinger investigators divided their study into retrospective and prospective sections. The algorithm was initially validated using a convolutional neural network that analyzed previously obtained CT images. This retrospective analysis, which looked at three-dimensional (3D) images, generated an AUC of 0.84 for predicting the presence or absence of ICH. During the second leg of the study, the researchers put the algorithm into a real-world prospective setting to speed up the evaluation of CT scans, part of a quality improvement initiative to help radiologists determine whether patients' scans required upgrading from

Health Catalyst DOS & Product Story – Animated Flow
Highly differentiated technology stack

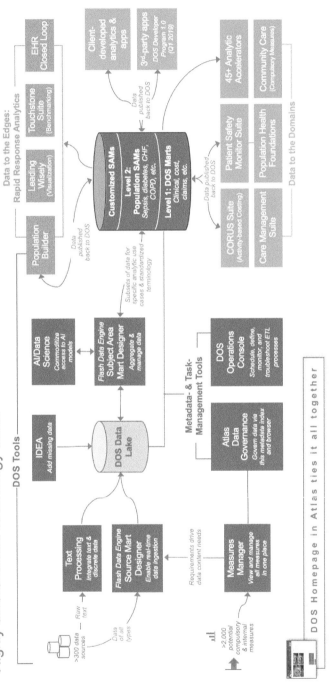

Figure 2.4A The Data Operating System combines the features of data warehouses, clinical data repositories, and health information exchanges and includes several key attributes that allow health systems to do a deeper dive into its at-risk patient populations and resurface with actionable insights. (Source: Health Catalyst, Salt Lake City, Utah. Reproduced with permission.)

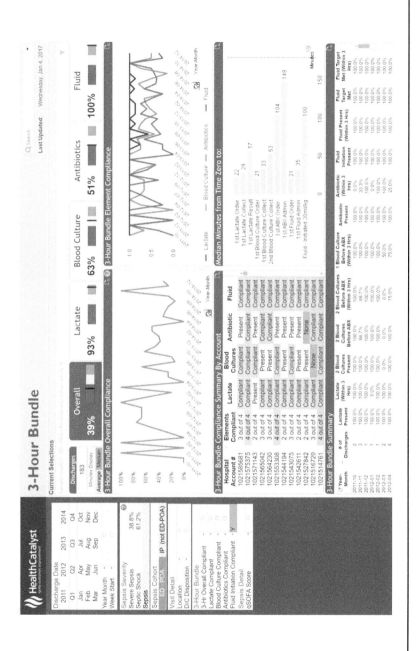

Figure 2.4B The Sepsis Prevention Analytics Application from Health Catalyst provides near real-time actionable data to help improve early recognition of sepsis, early intervention for severe sepsis, and early therapy for septic shock to reduce mortality. (*Source:* Health Catalyst, Salt Lake City, Utah. Reproduced with permission.)

routine to stat status. During this phase, 347 routine CT scans were evaluated with the ML algorithm, generating an accuracy rating of 84%, sensitivity 70%, and specificity 87%. Among these 347 scans, 94 needed to be upgraded to stat on radiologists' worklists (26%). Among the 94 cases, 60 had ICH according to the evaluating radiologist. The positive cases included 5 new outpatient ICH cases that normally would have remained in the "slow lane." Overall, the algorithm improved processing time, with stat scans being handled in 19 minutes (median time), compared to 512 minutes for routine studies.

Hyunkwang Lee, with the Massachusetts General Hospital Department of Radiology, and colleagues from Harvard University also employed a combination of retrospective and prospective approaches to develop and test their convolutional neural network model. Their goal, however, was to use the algorithm to specifically look for acute ICH.[51] The Lee et al. study also differed from the Geisinger study in 2 other aspects. They used a small data set, consisting of fewer than 1,000 patients, and they developed tools within the model to help explain the rationale of the algorithm's findings to non-experts, in the hope that they could address the black box issue that causes many clinicians to question the value of ML diagnostic aids. Despite the fact that the data set only used 904 cases to train the algorithm, it achieved a performance similar to what was accomplished by expert radiologists in two separate data sets: sensitivity 98%, specificity 95% among 200 cases; sensitivity 92%, specificity 95% in 196 cases. Lee et al. also state: "The system includes an attention map and a prediction basis retrieved from training data to enhance explainability, and an iterative process that mimics the workflow of radiologists."[51]

AI and Medication Management

Medication mismanagement continues to vex clinicians, policymakers, regulators, and the public. Among the most difficult management issues to contend with in the United States is the current opioid crisis. Numerous studies have documented the fact that surgical and dental patients are being overprescribed opioids after a procedure. Gabriel Brat, MD, an instructor in biomedical informatics at Harvard Medical School, and a trauma surgeon at BIDMC, and his colleagues, have summarized the statistics on the problem:

> *Overprescribing of opioids is thought to be a major contributor, where two thirds of opioid misuse can be attributed to opioids obtained through a single physician. Overprescribing enables opioid diversion and increases the potential for addiction. Surgical patients are nearly four times more likely to get post-discharge opioids than their non-surgical counterparts.*

Orthopedic surgeons alone were responsible for 7.7% of opioid prescriptions in 2009. Despite these numbers, surgeons have yet to find the right balance of opioid prescriptions: between 3% and 10% of opioid naive patients become chronic users, and emerging research suggests that as many as 80% of prescribed pills in the remaining group of patients are unused.[52]

Because there are no national guidelines for clinicians to follow when prescribing these medications, there is an urgent need to collect reliable statistics on what patients really need to manage their postoperative pain. Many large healthcare systems are developing locally relevant data and recommendations, but there is a need for more comprehensive, nationally accepted standards that can be personalized. Over the last few years, Beth Israel Deaconess Medical Center (BIDMC) in Boston has developed a database that used more than 7,000 surgical cases to determine the opioid dosages patients actually say they took after such procedures—based on phone, email, text, and in-person interviews with these patients postoperatively. Clinicians at BIDMC have access to this resource through a dashboard, illustrated in Figures 2.5A and 2.5B. As the figures indicate, the need for oxycodone ranges from 0 to 6 5-mg tablets after an uncomplicated appendectomy. The typical surgeon may order up to 30 tablets, however. Similarly, most patients say they only require 1–6 tablets after an uncomplicated cholecystectomy, despite the fact that surgeons usually order many more.

Brat and his associates have spearheaded the opioid management initiative. Brat points out that "surgeons have become part of the opioid crisis and they can be part of the solution. They dramatically overprescribe opioids."[52] His research team has collected data from thousands of patient interviews to document average postoperative opioid needs and develop the aforementioned database, and they have used that information to help surgeons at BIDMC and elsewhere. Since the initial project launched, several hospitals have formed a collaborative to pool their opioid-use data, which is now used to augment and expand the BIDMC database. A web application exists to serve as a reference to guide BIDMC surgeons' prescribing decisions, which will eventually become universally available.

The approach used by Gabriel Brat and his colleagues is promising, but there are other complementary approaches worth consideration. One of the challenges faced by clinicians is trying to decipher who is really at high risk for opioid misuse so that they can be targeted with preventive measures. It is customary to look at patients' dosage level, the number of pharmacies they have frequented, and the prescribing physician to estimate the likelihood that they are abusing opioids or will overdose on the medication. Unfortunately, these variables have proven less than optimal, in part because they fail to consider

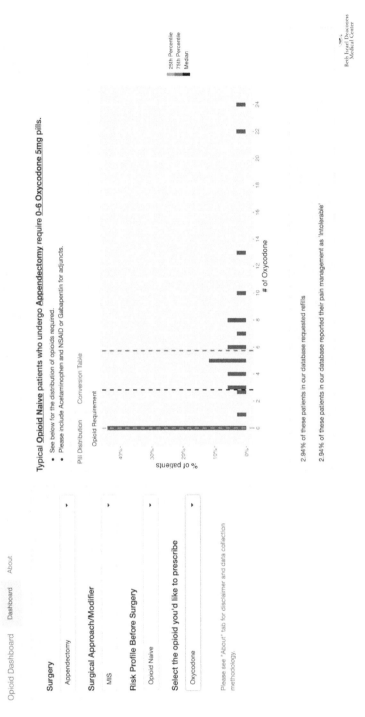

Figure 2.5A Patients typically require 0 to 6 5-mg tablets of oxycodone after an uncomplicated appendectomy. The dashboard gives surgeons access to this information and allows them to adjust the dosage based on several parameters, including the type of surgery, the patient's risk profile, and the specific opioid being prescribed. (Graphic courtesy of Gabriel Brat, MD, Beth Israel Deaconess Medical Center.)

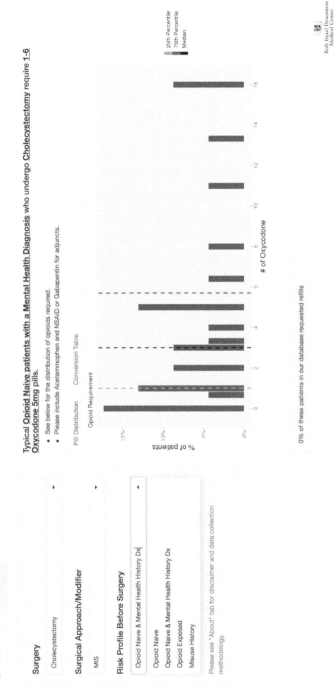

Figure 2.5B Most patients say they only require 1–6 tablets after an uncomplicated cholecystectomy. The dashboard gives surgeons access to this information and allows them to adjust the dosage based on several parameters. (Graphic courtesy of Gabriel Brat, MD, Beth Israel Deaconess Medical Center.)

several other potential risk factors, and because the standard statistical methods used to analyze these traditional risk factors fail to detect the complex interactions that may occur among the variables. Among the risk factors also worth consideration are trips to the ED, records that document the existence of psychiatric disease, various patient demographics, as well the specific characteristics and prescribing patterns of the prescribing clinician.

Machine learning has the potential to address this challenge by measuring a long list of possible risk factors, looking for a variety of unexpected interactions among them, and by detecting unique clusters of risk factors and unforeseen patterns. Wei-Hsuan Lo-Ciganic, PhD, with the Department of Pharmaceutical Outcomes and Policy at the University of Florida, and associates from other universities have analyzed the records of 500,000 non-cancer Medicare patients who had received at least one opioid prescription to look for such patterns, taking into account 268 predictors.[53] Their exhaustive retrospective study measured the total and mean daily morphine milligram equivalent (MME); cumulative and continuous duration of opioid use—which documents gaps of less than a month between prescription refills; the type of opioid drug and its duration of action; how many clinicians prescribed the medication and how many pharmacies filled the scripts; which patients refilled their script more than 3 days before it should have normally been used up; concurrent prescriptions of benzothiazines and muscle relaxants; whether patients were also taking methadone or buprenorphine for opioid use disorder; the patient's disability status and whether they are on a low-income subsidy; and their health status. The investigators also measured several characteristics of the prescribers including their specialty, how often they prescribe opioids and the dosage ordered, and the average monthly number of patients receiving the drugs.

To determine if a ML methodology was more useful than traditional statistical analysis, Lo-Ciganic et al. employed several analytical approaches with the ultimate aim of identifying how many patients had experienced a non-fatal or fatal opioid overdose. They included multivariate logistic regression, random forest modeling, gradient boosting machine (GBM), and deep neural networks.

As is customary with deep learning algorithm development, researchers created training, testing, and validation groups of Medicare patients, each containing over 186,000 individuals. The neural network–based and the GBM-based algorithms were more accurate in predicting beneficiaries who developed an overdose, when compared to the random forest–generated and logistic regression algorithms. And ML-based algorithms were also more useful in identifying patients who were very *unlikely* to experience an overdose. For instance, the team reported: "Using the GBM algorithm, 144,860 (77.6%) of the sample were categorized into low risk, 21,346 (11.4%) into medium risk, and 20,480 (11.0%)

into high risk for overdose. . . . Among all 91 beneficiaries with an overdose epi-sode in the sample, 69 (75.8%) were captured in the high-risk group. Similarly, using the DNN algorithm, 9747 individuals (5.2%) were predicted to be high risk, capturing 56 overdose episodes (61.5%). Among the 142,180 individuals (76.2%) categorized as low risk, 99.99% did not have an overdose."[53]

Another area of concern that is slowly responding to AI is polypharmacy. Far too many patients continue to take prescription medications that they no longer need, and too few clinicians are discontinuing these unnecessary and potentially harmful drugs. Considering the small window of opportunity that clinicians have to discuss medication management—the average office visit is less than 15 minutes—it is not surprising that polypharmacy has ballooned. Clinicians may also be wary of discontinuing a medication for fear that it may cause a patient's symptoms to reemerge, or worsen biomarkers that have improved. One way to address the problem of polypharmacy is by augment-ing physician services with pharmacist-assisted patient education.[54] Another is to document the existence of harmful drug/drug interactions. A Stanford University AI program called Decagon has the potential to address the second issue. The deep learning model created by Marinka Zitnik and colleagues ana-lyzed protein/protein interactions and drug/protein interactions that predict the side effects that can occur with specific 2-drug combinations.[55] With the help of a convolutional neural network, the Decagon program was found to be up to 69% more effective at predicting drug-interaction side effects than existing models. Decagon also found evidence suggesting 10 new drug interactions, 5 of which were confirmed by independent research.

It is clear from the aforementioned studies and commentary that ML will play a major role in decision making among clinicians, policy makers, and other stakeholders. The work that we presented here represents only a fraction of ML's potential. Other projects worth consideration include the use of ML classifiers to analyze EHR data to improve the diagnosis of pediatric disorders,[56] the use of convolutional neural networks in pneumonia screening,[57] and a CNN called CheXNeXt that may help radiologists better interpret chest X-rays to detect 14 different disorders.[58]

In the Final Analysis

In previous publications, we have discussed the relative strengths of various types of evidence, including meta-analyses, randomized clinical trials, big data analysis, and epidemiological studies.[41] Although many physicians and nurses believe that large-scale RCTs are the gold standard and remain near the top of the "strength of evidence" ladder, they also know from clinical experience that many diagnostic and therapeutic options are valuable despite the fact that they have yet to be confirmed with RCTs.

The AI and ML initiatives discussed above are supported by varying degrees of evidence. The software embedded in IDx-DR, for instance, is supported by prospective and retrospective studies. The system is now being used in several healthcare systems to screen patients for diabetic retinopathy. The software platforms used to distinguish skin cancer from benign moles has been validated in several retrospective data analyses in multiple countries, but to the best of our knowledge they have yet to be supported by prospective trials. The MD-Logic software incorporated in the DreaMed Advisor Pro platform, on the other hand, which is used to help patients with diabetes manage their disease, has been supported by at least two RCTs. Medial EarlySign's ColonFlag has also garnered considerable evidence in both retrospective and prospective studies, suggesting it can help reduce the incidence of colorectal cancer by detecting patients at risk at an early stage in the disease's development. AI- and ML-supported tools are by no means a panacea, as our next chapter will demonstrate, but there is every reason to believe they will play a major role in medicine's future.

References

1. "AI and Machine Learning: What Cuts Hype from Reality." *Healthcare IT News.* Retrieved on April 8, 2019.
2. Kaufman D. (2018, October 19). "Workers Beware: Algorithms Could Replace You—Someday." *The New York Times,* p. F2.
3. Rajkomar, A., Dean, J., and Kohane, I. (2019). "Machine Learning in Medicine." *New England Journal of Medicine,* vol. 380, pp. 1347–1354.
4. Brookings Institution. (2019, June 14). "What Is Artificial Intelligence?" Retrieved from https://www.brookings.edu/research/what-is-artificial-intelligence/
5. PBS Nova. "AI Explained; What Is a Neural Net?" Retrieved from https://www.youtube.com/watch?v=xS2G0oolHpo1358
6. Livingston, E. H. (2018). "Understanding How Machine Learning Works." Video supplement to "On the Prospects for a (Deep) Learning Health Care System." *JAMA,* vol. 320, pp. 1099–1100. Retrieved from https://edhub.ama-assn.org/jn-learning/video-player/16845576
7. Cerrato, P. and Halamka, J. (2019). *The Transformative Power of Mobile Medicine.* Cambridge (MA): Elsevier/Academic Press.
8. Naylor, C. D. (2018). "On the Prospects for a (Deep) Learning Health Care System." *JAMA,* vol. 320, pp. 1099–1100.
9. Gulshan, V., Peng, L., Coram, M., Stumpe, M. C., Wu, D., Narayanaswamy, A., Venugopalan, S., Widner, K., Madams, T., Cuadros, J., Kim, R., Raman,

R., Nelson, P. C., Mega, J. L., and Webster, D. R. (2016). "Development and Validation of a Deep Learning Algorithm for Detection of Diabetic Retinopathy in Retinal Fundus Photographs." *JAMA*, vol. 316, pp. 2402–2410.

10. "MEDCALC ROC Curve Analysis." Retrieved from https://www.medcalc.org/manual/roc-curves.php

11. U.S. Food and Drug Administration. (2018, April 11). "FDA Permits Marketing of Artificial Intelligence-Based Device to Detect Certain Diabetes-Related Eye Problems." Press release. Retrieved from https://www.fda.gov/news-events/press-announcements/fda-permits-marketing-artificial-intelligence-based-device-detect-certain-diabetes-related-eye

12. Abramoff, M. D., Lavin, P. T., Birch, M., Shah, N., and Folk, J. C. (2018). "Pivotal Trial of an Autonomous AI-Based Diagnostic System for Detection of Diabetic Retinopathy in Primary Care Offices." *Digital Medicine,* vol. 1, p. 39; http://doi.org/10.1038/s41746-018-0040-6.

13. Lin, H., Li, L., Liu, Z., Chen, J., Yang, J., Chen, H., and Lin, Z. (2019). "Diagnostic Efficacy and Therapeutic Decision-Making Capacity of an Artificial Intelligence Platform for Childhood Cataracts in Eye Clinics: A Multicentre Randomized Controlled Trial." *EClinical Medicine,* vol. 9, pp. 2–59.

14. Esteva, A., Kuprel, B., Novoa, R., Ko, J., Swetter, S. M., Blau, H. M., and Thrun, S. (2017). "Dermatologist-Level Classification of Skin Cancer with Deep Neural Networks." *Nature,* vol. 542, pp. 115–118.

15. Haenssle, H. A., Fink, C., Schneiderbauer, R., Toberer, F., Buhl, T., Blum, A., Kalloo, A., Hassen, A., Thomas, L., Enk, A., and Uhlmann, L. (2018). "Man against Machine: Diagnostic Performance of a Deep Learning Convolutional Neural Network for Dermoscopic Melanoma Recognition in Comparison to 58 Dermatologists." *Annals of Oncology,* vol. 29, pp. 1836–1842.

16. Brinker, T. J., Hekler, A., Enk, A. H., Klode, J., Hauschild, A., and Berking, C. (2019). "Deep Learning Outperformed 136 of 157 Dermatologists in a Head-to-Head Dermoscopic Melanoma Image Classification Task." *European Journal of Cancer,* vol. 113, pp. 47–54.

17. Yala, A., Lehman, C., Schuster, T., Portnoi, T., and Barzilay, R. (2019). "A Deep Learning Mammography-Based Model for Improved Breast Cancer Risk Prediction." *Radiology,* vol. 292, pp. 60–66; https://doi.org/10.1148/radiol.2019182716

18. Liu, Y., Kohlberger, T., Norouzi, M., Dahl, G. E., Smith, J. L., Mohtashamian, A., Olson, N., Peng, L. H., Hipp, J. D., and Stumpe, M. C. (2019). "Artificial Intelligence Based Breast Cancer Nodal Metastasis Detection." *Archives of Pathology & Laboratory Medicine*, vol. 143, pp. 859–868; http://doi.org/10.5858/arpa.2018-0147-OA

19. Steiner, D., MacDonald, R., Liu, Y., Truszkowski, P., Hipp, J. D., Gammage, C., Thng, F., Peng, L., and Stumpe, M. C. (2018). "Impact of Deep Learning Assistance on the Histopathologic Review of Lymph Nodes for Metastatic Breast Cancer." *American Journal of Surgical Pathology,* vol. 42, pp. 1636–1646.

20. Cruz-Roa, A., Gilmore, H., Basavanhally, A., Feldman, M., Ganesan, S., Shih, N., and Tomaszewski, J. (2017, April 18). "Accurate and Reproducible Invasive

Breast Cancer Detection in Whole Slide Images: A Deep Learning Approach for Quantifying Tumor Extent." *Scientific Reports,* vol. 7, p. 46450; http://doi.org/10.1038/srep46450

21. Bresnick, J. (2019, May 19). "Deep Learning Network 100% Accurate at Identifying Breast Cancer." *Health IT Analytics.* Retrieved on May 19, 2019, from https://healthitanalytics.com/news/deep-learning-network-100-accurate-at-identifying-breast-cancer

22. Hu, L., Bell, D., Antani, S., Xue, Z., Yu, K., Horning, M. P., Gachuhi, N., and Wilson, B. (2019). "An Observational Study of Deep Learning and Automated Evaluation of Cervical Images for Cancer Screening." *JNCI Journal of National Cancer Institute*; http://doi.org/10.1093/jnci/djy225

23. Gruetzemacher, R., Gupta, A., and Paradice, C. D. (2018). "3D Deep Learning for Detecting Pulmonary Nodules in CT Scans." *Journal of the American Medical Informatics Association,* vol. 25, no. 10, pp. 1301–1310.

24. Chilamkurthy, S., Ghosh, R., Tanamala, S., Biviji, M., Campeau, N. G., Venugopal, V. K., Mahajan, V., Rao, P, and Warier, P. (2018). "Deep Learning Algorithms for Detection of Critical Findings in Head CT Scans: A Retrospective Study." *Lancet,* vol. 392, no. 10162, pp. 2388–2396; http://doi.org/10.1016/S0140-6736(18)31645-3. Epub 2018 Oct 11

25. Byrne, M. F. and Shahidi, N. (2017). "Will Computer-Aided Detection and Diagnosis Revolutionize Colonoscopy?" *Gastroenterology,* vol. 153, pp. 1460–1464: e1.

26. Van Rijn, J. C., Reitsma, J. B., Stoker, J., Bossuyt, P. M., van Deventer, S. J., and Dekker E. (2006). "Polyp Miss Rate Determined by Tandem Colonoscopy: A Systematic Review." *American Journal of Gastroenterology,* vol. 101, pp. 343–350.

27. Wang, Y., Tavanapong, W., Wong, J., Oh, J. H., and de Groen, P. C. (2015). "Polyp-Alert: Near Real-Time Feedback during Colonoscopy." *Computer Methods and Programs in Biomedicine*, vol. 120, pp. 164–179.

28. Wang, P., Xiao, X., Brown, J. R., Berzin, T. M., Tu, M., Xiong, F., Hu, X., Liu, P., Song, Y., and Zhang, D. (2018). "Development and Validation of a Deep-Learning Algorithm for the Detection of Polyps during Colonoscopy." *Nature Biomedical Engineering,* vol. 2, pp. 741–748.

29. Hornbrook, M. C., Goshen, R., Choman, E., O'Keeffe-Rosetti, M., Kinar, Y., Liles, E. G., and Rust, K. C. (2017). "Early Colorectal Cancer Detected by Machine Learning Model Using Gender, Age, and Complete Blood Count Data." *Digestive Diseases and Sciences,* vol. 62, pp. 2719–2727.

30. Goshen, R., Choman, E., Ran, A., Muller, E., Kariv, R., Chodick, G., Ash, N., Narod, S., and Shalev, V. (2018, December). "Computer-Assisted Flagging of Individuals at High Risk of Colorectal Cancer in a Large Health Maintenance Organization Using the ColonFlag Test." *JCO Clinical Cancer Informatics*, vol. 2, pp. 1–8; http://doi.org/10.1200/CCI.17.00130

31. Hannun, A. Y., Rajpurkar, P., Haghpanahi, M., Tison, G. H., Bourn, C., Turakhia, M. P., and Ng, A. Y. (2019). "Cardiologist-Level Arrhythmia Detection and Classification in Ambulatory Electrocardiograms Using a Deep Neural Network." *Nature Medicine,* vol. 25, pp. 65–69.

32. Shah, A. P. and Rubin, S. A. (2007). "Errors in the Computerized Electro-cardiogram Interpretation of Cardiac Rhythm." *Journal of Electocardiology,* vol. 40, no. 5, pp. 385–390.

33. Banda, J., Sarraju, A., Abbasi, F., Parizo, J., Pariani, M., Ison, H., Briskin, E., Wand, H., Dubois, S., and Jung, K. (2019). "Finding Missed Cases of Familial Hypercholesterolemia in Health Systems Using Machine Learning." *Digital Medicine,* vol. 2, p. 23; https://doi.org/10.1038/s41746-019-0101-5

34. FDA. (2016). "Evaluation of Automatic Class III Designation for DreaMed Advisor Pro. Decision Summary." Retrieved on May 23, 2019, from https://www.accessdata.fda.gov/cdrh_docs/reviews/DEN170043.pdf

35. Philips, M., Battelino, T., Atlas, E., Kordonouri, O., Bratina, N., Miller, S., Biester, T., Stefanija, M. A., Muller, I., Nimri, R., and Danne, T. (2013). "Nocturnal Glucose Control with an Artificial Pancreas at a Diabetes Camp." *New England Journal of Medicine,* vol. 368, pp. 824–833.

36. Nimri, R., Muller, R., Atlas, E., Miller, S., Fogel, A., Bratina, N., and Kordonouri, O. (2014). "MD-Logic Overnight Control Got 6 Weeks of Home Use in Patients with Type 1 Diabetes: Randomized Crossover Trial." *Diabetes Care,* vol. 17, pp. 3025–3032.

37. Downing, J., Boolyky, J., and Schneider, J. (2017). "Use of a Connected Glucose Meter and Certified Diabetes Educator Coaching to Decrease the Likelihood of Abnormal Blood Glucose Excursions: The Livongo for Diabetes Program." *Journal of Medical Internet Research,* vol. 19, no. 7: e234.

38. Centers for Disease Control and Prevention. (2018, June 21). "Prediabetes: Your Chance to Prevent Type 2 Diabetes." Retrieved from https://www.cdc.gov/diabetes/basics/prediabetes.html

39. New York State Department of Health. (2017, February). "Prediabetes." Retrieved from https://www.health.ny.gov/diseases/conditions/diabetes/prediabetes/

40. Paruk, F. (2017, May 2). "New Analysis Reveals Higher Rates of Prediabetes Progressing to Diabetes." Allscripts. Retrieved from https://www.allscripts.com/news-insights/blog/blog/2017/05/new-analysis-reveals-higher-rates-of-prediabetes-progressing-to-diabetes

41. Centers for Disease Control and Prevention. (2018, August 10). "National Diabetes Prevention Program." Retrieved from https://www.cdc.gov/diabetes/prevention/index.html

42. Cerrato, P. and Halamka, J. (2017). *Realizing the Promise of Precision Medicine.* New York: Elsevier/Academic Press.

43. Medial EarlySign. (2017, November 1). "Medial EarlySign Machine Learning Algorithm Predicts Risk for Prediabetics Becoming Diabetic within 1 Year." Retrieved from http://us.earlysign.com/news-and-events/medial-earlysign-machine-learning-algorithm-predicts-risk-prediabetics-becoming-diabetic-within-1-year/

44. Komorowski, M., Celi, L. A., Badawi, O. O., Gordon A. C., and Faisal, A. A. (2018). "The Artificial Intelligence Clinician Learns Optimal Treatment Strategies for Sepsis in Intensive Care." *Nature Medicine,* vol. 24, pp. 1716–1720.

45. Shimabukuro, D. W., Barton, C. W., Feldman, M. D., Mataraso S. J, and Das, R.

(2017). "Effect of a Machine Learning-Based Severe Sepsis Prediction Algorithm on Patient Survival and Hospital Length of Stay: A Randomised Clinical Trial." *BMJ Open Respiratory Research,* vol. 4: e000234; http://doi.org/10.1136/bmjresp-2017-000234

46. Masino, A. J., Harris, M. C., Forsyth, D., Ostapenko, S., Srinivasan, L., Bonafide, C. P., Balamuth, F., Schmatz, M., and Grundmeier, R. W. (2019). "Machine Learning Models for Early Sepsis Recognition in the Neonatal Intensive Care Unit Using Readily Available Electronic Health Record Data." *PLoS One,* vol. 14, no. 2: e0212665; https://doi.org/10.1371/journal.pone.0212665

47. Desautels, T., Calvert, J., Hoffman, J., Jay, M., Kerem, Y., Shieh, L., Shimabukuro, D., Chettipally, U., Feldman, M. D., Barton, C., Wales, D. J., and Das, R. (2016). Prediction of Sepsis in the Intensive Care Unit with Minimal Electronic Health Record Data: A Machine Learning Approach." *JMIR Medical Informatics,* vol. 4: e28.

48. Seymour, C. W., Kennedy, J. N., Wang, S., Chang, C. H., Elliott, C. F., Xu, Z., Berry, S., Clermont, G., and Cooper, G. (2019). "Derivation, Validation, and Potential Treatment Implications of Novel Clinical Phenotypes for Sepsis." *JAMA,* vol. 321, pp. 2003–2017.

49. Health Catalyst. (2018, December 6). "Improving Identification of Hospitalized Patients with Sepsis." Retrieved from https://www.healthcatalyst.com/success_stories/inpatient-sepsis-care-mission-health

50. Arbabshirani, M. R., Fornwalt, B. K., Mongelluzzo, G., Suever, J. D., Geise, B. D., Patel, A. A., and Moore, G. J. (2018). "Advanced Machine Learning in Action: Identification of Intracranial Hemorrhage on Computed Tomography Scans of the Head with Clinical Workflow Integration." *Digital Medicine,* vol. 1, no. 9; http://doi.org/10.1038/s41746-017-0015-z

51. Lee, H., Yune, S., Mansouri, M., Kim, M., Tajmir, S. H., Guerrier, C. E., Ebert, S. A., and Pomerantz, S. R. (2019). "An Explainable Deep-Learning Algorithm for the Detection of Acute Intracranial Haemorrhage from Small Datasets." *Nature Biomedical Engineering,* vol. 3, pp. 173–182.

52. Brat, G., Agniel, D., Beam, A., Yorkgitis, B., Bicket, M., Homer, M., Fox, K. P., and Knecht, D. B. (2018). "Postsurgical Prescriptions for Opioid Naive Patients and Association with Overdose and Misuse: Retrospective Cohort Study." *BMJ,* vol. 360: j5790.

53. Lo-Ciganic, W.-H., Huang, J. L., Zhang, H. H., Weiss, J. C., Wu, Y., Kwoh, C. K., Donohue, J. M., Cochran, G., and Gordon, A. J. (2019). "Evaluation of Machine-Learning Algorithms for Predicting Opioid Overdose Risk Among Medicare Beneficiaries with Opioid Prescriptions." *JAMA Open,* vol. 2: e190968; http://doi.org/10.1001/jamanetworkopen.2019.0968

54. Martin, P., Tamblyn, R., Benedetti, A., Ahmed, S., and Tannenbaum, C. (2018). "Effect of a Pharmacist-Led Educational Intervention on Inappropriate Medication Prescriptions in Older Adults: The D-PRESCRIBE Randomized Clinical Trial." *JAMA,* vol. 320, pp. 1869–1898.

55. Zitnik, M., Agrawal, M., and Leskovec, J. (2018). "Modeling Polypharmacy

Side Effects with Graph Convolutional Networks." *Bioinformatics,* vol. 34, pp. i457–i466.

56. Liang, H., Tsui, B. Y., Ni, H., Valentim, C. C. S., Baxter, S. L., Liu, G., Cai, W., Kermany, D. S., Sun, X., Chen, J., He, L., and Zhu, J. (2019, March). Evaluation and Accurate Diagnoses of Pediatric Diseases Using Artificial Intelligence. *Nature Medicine,* vol. 25, no. 3, pp. 433–438; http://doi.org/10.1038/s41591-018-0335-9

57. Zech, J. R., Badgeley, M. A., Liu, M., Costa, A. B., Titano, J. J., and Oermann, E. K. (2018). "Variable Generalization Performance of a Deep Learning Model to Detect Pneumonia in Chest Radiographs: A Cross-Sectional Study." *PLOS Medicine,* vol. 15: e1002683; https://doi.org/10.1371/journal.pmed.1002683

58. Rajpurkar, P., Irvin, J., Ball, R. L., Zhu, K., Yang, B., Mehta, H., Duan, T., Ding, D., Bagul, A., and Langlotz, C. P. (2018, November 20). "Deep Learning for Chest Radiograph Diagnosis: A Retrospective Comparison of the CheXNeXt Algorithm to Practicing Radiologists." *PLOS Medicine,* vol. 15, no. 11: e1002686; http://doi.org/10.1371/journal.pmed.1002686

Chapter 3

AI Criticisms, Obstacles, and Limitations

In the last chapter, we discussed the promise of artificial intelligence (AI) and machine learning (ML). A recent survey of US physicians suggests that most physicians do not share this optimistic view and remain skeptical about these emerging digital tools. A Medscape survey of 1,500 doctors in the United States, Europe, and Latin America has found that only one 1 in 5 say AI has changed how they practice medicine, and 49% are anxious or uncomfortable about the role of AI in healthcare.[1] Nearly half of US respondents say, "I am uncomfortable and/or anxious about using AI-powered software." More than a third of physicians in Europe feel the same way, as do 30% of Latin Americans. Although the Medscape survey did not investigate the underlying reasons for such skepticism, the evidence points to several factors, including a lack of understanding on the part of clinicians about how the technology functions, the inability of many technologists to explain the mechanism of action of AI and ML in plain English, the poor quality of some data sets used to generate the algorithms, and the exaggerated claims of some AI enthusiasts.

Explainability Remains a Challenge

Clinicians are accustomed to using diagnostic and therapeutic tools they understand. They are not only interested in evidence to support the effectiveness and safety of these interventions but also want to know that the mechanism of action behind each of these interventions is plausible and consistent with the laws of nature governing human physiology and biochemistry. Unfortunately, throughout the course of history, this need for plausibility has sometimes meant rejecting treatment options that work but are inconsistent with the theories in vogue at the time. In 1860, for example, the Hungarian physician Ignaz Semmelweis published a seminal work demonstrating that puerperal fever was caused by some sort of "putrid" matter that was being transferred from the hands of medical students who had just finished examining cadavers to pregnant women during their physical examination. Few authorities at the time took his findings seriously because he could not provide a plausible mechanism of action that was consistent with the theories of the day.

Conversely, while resistance to effective interventions that challenge conventional wisdom has slowed down their acceptance in medical practice in many cases, there are also examples of treatments that have been widely accepted even though they lack a proven biological mechanism. Aspirin has been prescribed to relieve pain for 100 years, even though the mechanism of action was only discovered recently. Similarly, the benefits of lithium for the management of bipolar disease have been well documented, but we still do not fully understand why. The history of puerperal fever, aspirin, and lithium suggest it may be possible to get clinicians' buy-in for AI and ML tools in three ways: (1) generate the kind of definitive evidence of clinical effectiveness that simply cannot be ignored; (2) provide clinicians with better explanations in plain English; and (3) educate them on the ABCs of information technology (IT) at the training stage of their careers and through continuing medical education. Convincing evidence for the effectiveness of healthcare IT in direct patient care is slowly emerging, as we discussed in Chapter 2. The need for simple explanations of how neural networks and other ML tools work is being addressed by online tutorials, including educational videos such as the one hosted by Edward H. Livingston, MD, in which he explains how a convolutional neural network (CNN) works.[2]

The tutorial explains that CNNs allow computers to analyze and classify data, including visual images, through several steps referred to as layers. In the example that Livingston uses, the images are more than 100,000 retinal scans that were analyzed by Google scientists to help the CNN algorithm distinguish between a normal retina and one that suggests the presence of diabetic retinopathy.[3] Using simple graphics, a *JAMA* video opens up the mysterious black box to explain how the system works. A CNN is a series of analytic processes that are organized into layers. With each layer, the CNN progresses from detecting simpler to more complex features in the image. It performs this feat by using software "filters." Images are composed of a variety of structures, including curves, corners, color variations, textures and so on. The filters are "constituting little miniature versions of each of these little building blocks," explains Lawrence Carin, PhD, in the tutorial. The neural network looks for these building blocks through the process of convolution, a mathematical operation in which filters walk through the image looking for specific features. The filter can be compared to a stencil that is passed over a photograph. As it passes over the image, certain parts of the image stand out—depending on what has been cut out of the stencil—and become visible.

Livingston uses the analogy of a written document to clarify the process. A document is composed of paragraphs, which in turn are made up of sentences, words, and letters. "Reading a document requires assessing the relationship of letters to one another in increasing layers of complexity." This hierarchy is similar to the hierarchy in a CNN. In layer one of the network, the filter looks for basic building blocks of the image, just as we might look for individual letters in a text document if we were trying to identify a person's name. In the video, the name the computer is trying to decipher is Ada Lovelace—a well-known figure in the history of AI. As the stencils pass over parts of the document, the stencil of the letter "A" will pick out all the corresponding As in her name, placing them on a feature map in the CNN, which then becomes part of a specific layer (see Figure 3.1). Gradually, additional layers are formed as filters of other letters pick out other parts of her name.

A CNN that analyzes a medical image of the retina would be looking at pixels rather than letters, words, and sentences. The first few layers of the CNN might encode for combinations of pixels that indicate the existence of a lesion's edges or other unique features. As the layers are stacked up, eventually the system can detect bleeding and microaneurysms, and at the end of the process, the CNN will combine all the data and make a final prediction: retinopathy, or no retinopathy.

Although well-crafted video tutorials are one way to convince reluctant clinicians to embrace AI-enhanced algorithms, they are by no means the only way. Another option is to build an understandable rationale into the neural network itself. For instance, when a CNN identifies a specific medical image that it tags as retinopathy, it can visually highlight those sections of the image that it has found to be indicative of the disease, thus giving clinicians the opportunity to inspect that portion of the image and see the algorithm's justification for labeling it as retinopathy. Michael Wainberg, with Deep Genomics, Inc., and his colleagues from Stanford University's Department of Computer Science, take this strategy a step further by pointing out that: "Such regions can be computed by sensitivity analysis, asking 'What perturbation to this image would change its diagnosis?' Deep learning provides the computational machinery to answer this question . . ."[4]

Figure 3.1 The filters in a convolutional neural network (CNN) act like stencils that recognize specific portions of the image when they pass over it. When the filter detects a matching element in the image—an "A" in this analogy—the convolution process generates a strong signal. That signal, in turn, is mapped onto a feature map.

Wainberg et al. also offered the following wisdom on addressing the skepticism and caution of others:

> *Assumptions should not be made about what constitutes a good rationale or causal explanation. Instead, it is important to study stakeholders and engage them in advance, by listening, teaching and learning, to establish expectations. . . . It should be kept in mind that a good rationale is one that holds up to adversarial challenges, in which the assumptions, intermediate conclusions and causal variables are poked and prodded, often from different perspectives, especially ones that were not incorporated into the training procedure. Stakeholders often gain confidence through interaction, by asking unexpected questions to see if the model's decision can be rationalized from different perspectives. For this purpose, it may be necessary to support interactive testing with stakeholders, including the ability to produce hypotheses and to test them experimentally.*[4]

Although highlighting specific regions in a medical image can help convince clinicians that an algorithm's outputs are reasonable, when the algorithm is not based on the analysis of images, there are other options that will promote explainability. If a ML-based algorithm is derived from electronic health record (EHR) data that includes free text entries in patient records, highlighting those sections of the record that were used to arrive at a prediction for individual patients can go a long way toward convincing clinicians of the rationale behind the algorithm. Seeing key portions of a patient's history combined with their radiology findings will probably be more persuasive than citing the mathematical equations used to develop the algorithm.[5]

Earlier in this chapter, we emphasized the need to educate clinicians on the ABCs of IT at the training stage of their careers. Unfortunately, research suggests that healthcare IT (HIT) has yet to make significant inroads into the medical school curriculum, although this is slowly changing.[6] Those changes align with a growing awareness in the medical community of the need for such education. A survey conducted by the Deliotte Center for Health Solutions found that 81% of physicians believe that HIT and EHR tools were essential for the physician of the future to practice successfully.[7] The same report went on to state: "Many medical schools have also begun to integrate HIT systems into physician education. In health systems and medical schools with shared databases and technologically integrated care, physicians in training will increasingly have the ability to use HIT for real-time decision support. One application in the future is to use HIT to support care management and case management, as well as to improve transitions—applying lessons learned from inpatient care to other settings."

Generalizability Remains Elusive

Conventional clinical trials have often been criticized for producing results that only apply to the population sample that was studied in the trial. Such trials typically include several inclusion and exclusion criteria that limit the generalizability of their results. They may restrict the study population to males between 18 and 50 years of age, for instance, or avoid patients with co-existing disorders. This generalizability problem can be just as high a hurdle for deep learning algorithms.

In Chapter 2, we summarized the research of Juan Banda and his colleagues, who developed a ML system to help identify patients most likely to have familial hypercholesterolemia.[8] To address the generalizability issue, developers tested their software on 2 completely separate data sets, namely, EHR data from Stanford Health Care patients and on patients from the Geisinger Healthcare System. Not every ML project has been this thorough in vetting its platform. John Zech, California Pacific Medical Center in San Francisco, and his associates, developed a CNN to screen for pneumonia across 3 hospital systems using large data sets of X-ray images from the National Institutes of Health Clinical Center, Mount Sinai Hospital (MSH), and the Indiana University Network for Patient Care (IU).[9] They found that, "When models were trained on pooled data from sites with different pneumonia prevalence, they performed better on new pooled data from these sites but not on external data," the result of overfitting. Similarly, if a CNN is developed to estimate who is at risk of being emergently admitted to a hospital, it may rely on data from past admissions of patients, namely, patients who have a specific set of symptoms, demographics, and so on. But in the real world, if those modeling features differ significantly from the characteristics of the hospital population one is trying to apply the CNN to—including bed availability, ethnic background, and insurance carriers—the predictions may be inaccurate for individual patients.[10]

The black box and generalizability problems have become serious enough to warrant the attention of several stakeholder organizations. The Clinical Decision Support Coalition (CDSC), a group that includes software developers, patient advocacy organizations, healthcare providers and payers, and clinical societies, has issued guidelines to address these issues.[11] CDSC's guidelines state: "Software built on machine learning needs to explain that it has spotted an association through machine learning, and state as precisely as it can the association. For example, with regard to a particular patient, the software might note that there is an association between patients with X, Y, and Z symptoms and improvements in those symptoms when taking Drug A."

The organization has also issued 5 steps for developers to adhere to as they design ML systems: First, the software should be straightforward about explaining its rationale, when possible. Second, the quality of the source used to generate the algorithm should be stated, as well as any information that will allow users to judge its quality. Third, developers should explain the data sets used to develop the platform. Fourth, developers should state the confidence level for reaching the recommendation provided by the software. Last, the CDSC encourages developers to "state the association as precisely as possible."

ML systems only establish associations between inputs and outputs, for example, between a specific set of visual features on a dermatologic image and the conclusion that it is a melanoma or a normal mole. But such associations, although they do not definitively establish cause and effect relationships, should not necessarily turn clinicians away. After all, many routine interventions in clinical medicine are also based on associations but lack well-documented causality.

The Petrie-Flom Center for Health Law Policy, Biotechnology, and Bioethics at Harvard Medical School has partnered with the University of Copenhagen's Center for Advanced Studies in Biomedical Innovation Law on a project that will examine the ethical and legal implications of AI and ML.[12,13] It, too, is interested in investigating the ramifications of what it describes as "black-box precision medicine," which includes the ML algorithms discussed earlier in the book. The project raises legitimate concerns about the verity of software systems that recommend changes in insulin dosage, for example, but do not have enough evidence to support these recommendations.

The Harvard/University of Copenhagen project certainly has good reason to question the accuracy and plausibility of some AI-based programs. A case in point is the so-called AI diet. In a recent *New York Times* article, Eric Topol, MD, a cardiologist with the Scripps Clinic, described a 2-week experiment in which he participated, with the goal of creating a more individualized diet regimen. With the help of ML tools developed by Eran Segal and his colleagues at the Weizmann Institute of Science, Topol used his smartphone to monitor his food and beverage intake as well as sleeping and exercise habits. Sensors measured his blood glucose levels, and a stool sample was obtained to measure his gut microbiome.[14] The results of the analysis were unexpected: "Cheesecake was given an A grade, but whole-wheat fig bars were a C−. In fruits: Strawberries were an A+ for me, but grapefruit a C. In legumes: Mixed nuts were an A+, but veggie burgers a C. . . . For the most part, the highly recommended foods, like cheese danishes, were ones I really disliked, while those rated C−, like oatmeal, melon and baked squash, were typically among my favorites. Bratwurst (the worst and potentially most lethal kind of food in my perception) was rated an A+!"

Although Topol admits that the technology upon which these recommendations were based will require randomized clinical trials before it should be fully implemented, he nonetheless remained enthusiastic about its potential to help consumers move away from a one-size-fits-all approach to nutrition planning that is more personalized. The problem with the technology and the dietary recommendations, however, is that they *ignore* decades of scientific research demonstrating the harm done by saturated fat and refined sugar. Some may argue that the value of ML is that it challenges conventional wisdom and fosters innovation, but the AI diet doesn't just challenge conventional wisdom, it overlooks good science. Clinical and epidemiological research have proven that a nutritional plan that focuses on unprocessed foods low in saturated fat and refined sugar reduces the risk of heart disease and obesity. And less obesity translates into a lower risk of Type 2 diabetes.

Addressing Hype, Fraud, and Misinformation

The accuracy of ML-enabled software is also on the minds of stakeholders concerned about bad actors and scam artists who may alter or slant content in a data set. It is now possible to add a few visually undetectable pixels to a medical image and trick an algorithm into misinterpreting a normal mole as a melanoma, for example.[15] By rotating images being analyzed by a CNN, it is also possible to alter the software's outputs. Additionally researchers have demonstrated that malware can be used to change three-dimensional (3D) CT data to inject or remove evidence of lung cancer. The same investigators were able to intercept and alter CT scans in an active hospital system as part of a security penetration test.[16] How might such manipulated data be used by unethical hackers? One option is to use it to influence a national election by giving a candidate a life-threatening disease. Another possibility is to change the vast majority of medical images in a hospital's data set and then hold the unaltered data for ransom.

Another malicious option to be concerned about: Choosing one synonym over another in an algorithm powered by natural language processing can influence how it determines the risk of misusing opioids. Similarly, Finlayson et al.[15] point out that it is possible to influence insurance reimbursement decisions by using adversarial techniques "to automate the discovery of code combinations that maximize reimbursement or minimize the probability of claims rejection. . . . Adversarial methods could allow billing teams to scale up upcoding practices without getting flagged by fraud detectors." Of course, it is not hard to imagine how insurance companies themselves might create algorithms that minimize the amount of money they spend on medical claim reimbursements. There is no simple way to eliminate these adversarial attacks, but one partial solution is for healthcare providers to create a fingerprint hash of "virgin" data that is likely to be manipulated, storing it, and then comparing it to data from a suspect algorithm to look for tampering.

Unfortunately, even algorithm developers with good intentions can take a wrong turn, or exaggerate the power of their services and products. A case in point is the missteps taken by IBM Watson as it attempted to use its super-computer and software to improve cancer care. By most accounts, the company has not accomplished that lofty goal. When IBM launched its oncology-related services, several cancer centers signed on, including Memorial Sloan Kettering in New York and MD Anderson Cancer Center in Texas. To investigate IBM's claims and its performance at several hospitals, *STAT News* interviewed dozens of physicians, IBM experts, AI specialists, and others. The investigators concluded: "The interviews suggest that IBM, in its rush to bolster flagging revenue, unleashed a product without fully assessing the challenges of deploying it in hospitals globally. Although it has emphatically marketed Watson for cancer care, IBM hasn't published any scientific papers demonstrating how the technology affects physicians and patients. As a result, its flaws are getting exposure on the front lines of care by doctors and researchers who say that the system, while promising in some respects, remains undeveloped."[17]

Critics say that IBM's overreach has been the result of letting its marketing claims get ahead of its clinical capabilities. The plan was to collect massive amounts of information about how to best treat various types of cancer from physicians' notes, the scientific literature, and from clinical guidelines. That approach was supposed to result in important insights and new approaches to the disorder. The initiative has been so disappointing that MD Anderson has cancelled its partnership with Watson for oncology.

Since *STAT News* conducted its initial investigation in 2017, it has gained access to internal IBM documents, which revealed that: "The software was drilled with a small number of 'synthetic' cancer cases, or hypothetical patients, rather than real patient data. Recommendations were based on the expertise of a few specialists for each cancer type, the documents say, instead of 'guidelines or evidence.'"[18]

Combating AI Bias

Any discussion of AI limitations and obstacles must include a discussion of bias as well. Some algorithms are derived from data collections that are too small or do not represent the cultural, racial, and socioeconomic status of the patient population they are trying to serve. Data sets derived from a hospital's EHR content may be skewed in the wrong direction if they are based solely on inpatient data and are trying to make predictions about ambulatory patient outcomes. Similarly, data sets that rely too heavily on male patients are likely to misrepresent the needs of female patients. And if an algorithm is created from a group of patients who have been treated in a clinic and then applied to a population cared for in private office practices, that can generate misleading results as well—no matter how large the data set used to generate the software.

Many ML-based algorithms are predictive in nature and assign a risk score to patients most likely to develop a disorder or develop complications for a disease they already have. But the precision of these risk scores depends on the number of patients in the data set as well as the demographic and other characteristics described in the repository. This creates a significant disadvantage for patient subgroups who are underrepresented. For example, if too few African Americans are included in a data set, but African Americans' risk of developing renal complications from diabetes is 10 times greater than the risk of white patients, a predictive algorithm is less likely to flag a black patient whose renal status is deteriorating. Milena A. Gianfrancesco, PhD, with the University of California, San Francisco, and her colleagues raise a similar concern:

> *When an algorithm cannot observe and identify certain individuals, a machine learning model cannot assign an outcome to them. Although the degree to which race/ethnicity, socioeconomic status, and related variables are missing in the electronic health record is not known, most commercial insurance plans are missing at least half of their data on ethnicity, primary spoken language, and primary written language; only one-third of commercial plans reported complete and partially complete data on race, patterns that are likely reflected in electronic health record data.*[19]

Our analysis clearly demonstrates that AI and ML hold promise, but we will still have to overcome a long list of limitations and obstacles before they are fully integrated into the healthcare ecosystem. Considering the potential of these digital tools and the growing number of providers, investors, and entrepreneurs currently committing their resources to the effort, it's only a matter of time before this happens.

References

1. Frellick, M. (2019, May 6). "AI Use in Healthcare Increasing Slowly Worldwide." Medscape. Retrieved from https://www.medscape.com/viewarticle/912629
2. Livingston, E. H. (2018). "Understanding How Machine Learning Works." Video supplement to "On the Prospects for a (Deep) Learning Health Care System." *JAMA*, vol. 320, pp. 1099–1100. Retrieved from https://edhub.ama-assn.org/jn-learning/video-player/16845576
3. Gulshan, V, Peng, L., Coram, M., Stumpe, M. C., Wu, D., Narayanaswamy, A., Venugopalan, S., Widner, K., Madams, T., and Cuadros, J. (2016). "Development

and Validation of a Deep Learning Algorithm for Detection of Diabetic Retinopathy in Retinal Fundus Photographs." *JAMA*, vol. 316, pp. 2402–2410.

4. Wainberg, M., Merico, D., Delong, A., and Frey, B. J. (2018). "Deep Learning in Biomedicine." *Nature Biotechnology,* vol. 36, pp. 829–838.

5. Rajkomar, A., Oren, E., Chen, K., Dai, A. M., Hajaj, N., and Hardt, M. (2018). "Scalable and Accurate Deep Learning with Electronic Health Records." *Digital Medicine*, vol. 1, p. 18; https://doi.org/10.1038/s41746-018-0029-1

6. Malik, H. and Hossain, I. T. (2015). "Healthcare Information Technology in Medical Education—A Forgotten Focus." *Medical Education Online*, vol. 20; https://doi.org/10.3402/meo.v20.30191.

7. Abrams, K. and Kane, A. (2016, April 5). "Preparing the Doctor of the Future: Medical School and Residency Program Evolution." *Deloitte Insights*. Retrieved from https://www2.deloitte.com/insights/us/en/industry/health-care/doctor-of-the-future-medical-school-residency-programs.html

8. Banda, J., Sarraju, A., Abbasi, F., Parizo, J., Pariani, M., and Ison, H. (2019). "Finding Missed Cases of Familial Hypercholesterolemia in Health Systems Using Machine Learning." *Digital Medicine*, vol. 2, p. 23; https://doi.org/10.1038/s41746-019-0101-5

9. Zech, J. R., Badgeley, M. A., Liu, M., Costa, A. B., Titano, J. J., and Oermann, E. C. (2018). "Variable Generalization Performance of a Deep Learning Model to Detect Pneumonia in Chest Radiographs: A Cross-Sectional Study." *PLOS Medicine*, vol. 15: e1002683; https://doi.org/10.1371/journal.pmed.1002683

10. Saria, S., Butte, A., and Sheikh, A. (2018). "Better Medicine through Machine Learning: What's Real, and What's Artificial?" *PLoS Medicine,* vol. 15, no. 12: e1002721.

11. Clinical Decision Support Coalition. (2017, August 30). "Introductory Memorandum." Retrieved from http://cdscoalition.org/wp-content/uploads/2017/08/CDS-3060-Guidelines-Final-2.pdf

12. Bresnick, J. (2018, February 2). "Can Healthcare Avoid "Black Box" Artificial Intelligence Tools?" *Health IT Analytics.* Retrieved from https://healthitanalytics.com/news/can-healthcare-avoid-black-box-artificial-intelligence-tools

13. Petrie-Flom Center. (2018, January 23). "The Petrie-Flom Center Launches New Project: Precision Medicine, Artificial Intelligence, and the Law (PMAIL)." Retrieved from https://petrieflom.law.harvard.edu/resources/article/petrie-flom-center-launches-pmail-project

14. Topol, E. (2019, March 2). "The A.I. Diet: Forget Government-Issued Food Pyramids. Let an Algorithm Tell You How to Eat." *The New York Times.*

15. Finlayson, S. G., Bowers, J. D., Ito, J., Zittrain, J. I., Beam, A. L., and Kohane, I. S. (2019). "Adversarial Attacks on Medical Machine Learning." *Science*, vol. 363, pp. 1287–1289.

16. Mirsky, Y., Mahler, T., Shelef, I., and Elovicit, Y. (2019, January 11). "CT-GAN: Malicious Tampering of 3D Medical Imagery Using Deep Learning. Proceedings of the 28th USENIX Security Symposium (USENIX Security 2019)." Retrieved from https://arxiv.org/abs/1901.03597

17. Ross, C. and Swetlitz, I. (2017, September 5). "IBM Pitched Its Watson Super-computer as a Revolution in Cancer Care. It's Nowhere Close." *STAT.* Retrieved from https://www.statnews.com/2017/09/05/watson-ibm-cancer/
18. Ross, C. and Swetlitz, I. (2018, July 25). "IBM's Watson Supercomputer Recommended 'Unsafe and Incorrect' Cancer Treatments, Internal Documents Show." *Stat News.* Retrieved from https://www.statnews.com/2018/07/25/ibm-watson-recommended-unsafe-incorrect-treatments/
19. Gianfrancesco, M., Tamang, S., Yazdany, J., and Schmajuk, G. (2018). "Potential Biases in Machine Learning Algorithms Using Electronic Health Record Data." *JAMA Internal Medicine,* vol. 178, pp. 1544–1547.

Chapter 4

CDS Systems: Past, Present, and Future

As stated in Chapter 1, although our primary theme is reinventing clinical decision support, there is no need to reinvent the wheel. There is much that can be done to reduce the number of diagnostic errors and to improve clinical decision making that does not require the latest innovations in artificial intelligence (AI), machine learning (ML), and data analytics. But a careful look at the research on currently available clinical decision support (CDS) systems also reveals that there is much to *dislike* about these tools, and much that does, in fact, need to be reimagined, reinvented, and reengineered.

CDS Has Improved Dramatically Over Time

But before exploring these issues, it is important to recognize the progress that has already been made in developing CDS tools over the last few decades. By 1990, CDS existed in some hospital settings to help with quality control, document scanning, and research, and in office practice, digital systems were mostly limited to practice management and to administrative functioning. Support for clinical decision making was rare.[1] There was also a paucity of standardized clinical terminology available to allow seamless communication between electronic information systems. Over time, this deficiency has been addressed with the development of standards such as Logical Observation Identifiers Names and Codes (LOINC), Systematized Nomenclature of Medicine (SNOMED), procedural codes such as Current Procedural Terminology (CPT), and standardized nomenclature for drug names, for example, RxNorm.

Although clinicians complain about the lack of user friendliness of electronic health record (EHR) systems, near universal adoption of EHRs across the US healthcare system was likewise an essential precursor for currently available CDS tools to accomplish what they already have. Without the patient data available in an EHR, clinicians would have to manually type in all the demographics, lab values, and other essentials used by a CDS system to arrive at useful recommendations. Similarly, although many practitioners want to see better integration of CDS systems into their workflow, most systems were completely standalone in the 1990s. Today, many EHR vendors have folded CDS tools into their products.

Today's CDS systems also benefit from knowledge bases that extract recommendations from meta-analyses, systematic literature reviews, and national clinical guidelines; these assets were not widely available in earlier decades. And although interoperability remains a work in progress, we have come a long way since the 1990s.

How Effective Are CDS Systems?

The evidence to show that CDS systems improve clinical outcomes is mixed. For example, CDS tools used to help clinicians manage a patient's cardiovascular risks have had little impact on improving systolic blood pressure, low-density lipoprotein levels, and hemoglobin A1c levels, with the exception of LDL levels in patients with diabetes. However, a meta-analysis of 22 studies published in 2019 found that integrating a CDS system into an EHR system did improve its effectiveness in managing cardiovascular risks.[2]

An older systematic review of CDS systems, published in 2005, found that about two thirds of the programs improved clinical practice (68%), which means, of course, that a third had no significant impact.[3] Certain software features improved the effective of these systems. Folding the CDS tool into clinicians' workflow had the most significant impact on its usefulness ($P < 0.00001$). Other features that improved clinical value included the provision of recommendations rather than just assessments, and giving clinicians advice at the opportune time, namely, at the time and in the location in which the decision making took place.

A more recent analysis (2017) suggests that overall CDS systems have not improved that much in the last 12 years: 29% had no effect on patient outcomes and 1 had a negative impact.[4] But on a more positive note, among the 70 studies included in the review, 7% found systems reduced mortality, 23% lowered the rate of life-threatening events, and 40% reduced non–life-threatening events. Those clinical areas that experienced the most meaningful benefits included "blood glucose management, blood transfusion management, physiologic deterioration prevention, pressure ulcer prevention, acute kidney injury prevention, and venous thromboembolism prophylaxis."

When we analyze studies that look specifically at the effect of CDS systems on patient-reported outcomes (PROs), the evidence is less encouraging. Among 15 studies that evaluated PROs, only 3 reported positive effects using computerized CDS systems.[5] David Blum, with the Norwegian University of Science and Technology in Trondheim, and his colleagues defined PROs as either improvement in patients' symptoms or quality of life. In one of the positive studies, clinical guidelines from a CDS system allowed practitioners to mitigate acute exacerbations in patients with asthma, when compared to patients managed by practitioners who did not have access to the system (17% vs. 8%). Similarly, psychiatrists treating schizophrenic patients saw better results when they had access to national guidelines through an EHR-based CDS system. Patients also experienced fewer re-hospitalizations.

A review of randomized controlled trials (RCTs) that looked specifically at the role of CDS systems in diabetes care likewise produced mixed findings.[6] Research has demonstrated that clinicians often ignore diabetes care standards, and it was hoped that CDS systems that gave them easy access to these standards would improve compliance. The systematic review analyzed 8 trials and 17 clinical markers. Although the investigators did find that CDS tools significantly improved clinicians' adherence to recommended guidelines, that adherence had a limited effect on quality of care and patient outcomes. For instance, in 4 of the trials analyzed, testing for hemoglobin A1c improved; several studies reported weak to modest improvements in glycated HbA1c levels among patients. Annual LDL cholesterol testing also increased in some of reported trials, but once again, clinical outcomes were only modestly better in CDS system-monitored patients compared to controls. At least one trial found that patients monitored with a CDS system were more likely to have their blood pressure checked, and 2 trials reported better blood pressure readings. Overall, the weak to modest improvements in process of care metrics and clinical outcomes were partially the result of the consistently low adoption of the CDS technology by practitioners who were exposed to it.

Investigators have also tried to determine how effective CDS systems are in recommending advanced imaging studies for Medicare patients. They analyzed over 117,000 orders for magnetic resonance imaging (MRI), computed tomography (CT), and nuclear medicine procedures that were processed through computerized physician order systems by more than 3,000 clinicians from 8 states, including academic medical centers, integrated delivery systems, and independent medical practices.[7] The CDS systems under review had been programmed with criteria developed by expert panels that had studied the relevant evidence and developed a set of appropriateness standards and a structured rating process.

Unfortunately, Hussey et al.[7] found that the CDS systems could not tell clinicians whether the test procedure they were ordering were appropriate or not 66.5% of the time.

Despite the mixed reviews of CDS systems, the US Centers for Disease Control and Prevention (CDC) maintains a positive view of these tools, stating that CDS "is an effective strategy for increasing the quality of care in screening, testing, and treating patients with high blood pressure and high cholesterol. Evidence that it directly affects health outcomes is lacking." More specifically, the CDC analysis found that the reminders generated by these tools help increase recommendations to patients to go for blood pressure and cholesterol screening and encourage preventive care, including smoking cessation.[8]

Obstacles to CDS Implementation and Effectiveness

If there ever was a reason to reinvent CDS tools, clinicians' less than enthusiastic embrace is certainly near the top of the list. One of the recurrent complaints by physicians and nurses who use these software systems is the fact that they often interfere with their workflow. Either the tools do not appear at the appropriate time during the diagnostic process or when a decision has to be made about treatment choices, or they require clinicians to move outside the EHR system they are using to gain access to the CDS system. Even more disruptive are all the electronic alerts that interfere with their thought process and require that they go in a different direction.[9]

Problems with workflow can be added to a long list of objections that slow down clinicians' use of CDS systems. They also question whether the expert advice built into their system is valid; others believe using these tools makes them less efficient. Another objection comes from practitioners who have found the information too obvious; in other words, they already know what the CDS system is telling them, which is why they find such alerts so annoying. Figure 4.1 outlines these criticisms in more detail and also lists positive opinions about these tools. Negative views outnumber positive views.

The alert fatigue problem remains a thorn in the side of clinicians and CDS vendors alike. Clinicians are sometimes bombarded with so many alerts that it distracts them from direct patient care. And vendors still struggle to design software solutions that will let clinicians see only the most relevant alerts. According to one estimate, physicians override or ignore between 49% and 96%

Table 1

Summary of user acceptance related to clinical decision support systems (CDSSs) from previous studies (N=11).

Study	Favorable response to CDSS	Unfavorable response to CDSS	CDSS Description
Bergman & Fors (2005) [15]	Can save time and provide structure	Not suitable to workflow and there is the risk of becoming dependent	CDSS for medical diagnosis of psychiatric diseases
Curry & Reed (2011) [16]	Concept was supported	Interference with workflow and questionable validity	Prompts for adhering to diagnostic imaging guidelines
Gadd et al (1998) [18]	Easy to use, limits the need for data entry, accurate, and relevant	Benefits are lost because it takes so long to use	Internet-based system that interactively presents clinical practice guidelines at point of care
Johnson et al (2014) [19]	Longitudinal acceptance behavior, perceived ease of use, and perceived usefulness	Computer literacy, user satisfaction, and general optimism	Clinical reminders and alerts for patients with asthma, diabetes, hypertension, and hyperlipidemia
Rosenbloom et al (2004) [20]	Can improve efficiency and quality of care; enhances education	Senior physicians did not think it was necessary	CDSS for computerized order entry system
Rousseau et al (2003) [21]	Use of "active" CDSS can bridge the gap between own practice and best practice	Clinicians found it to be difficult to use and unhelpful clinically	CDSS for chronic disease in general practice
Shibl et al (2013) [22]	Performance expectancy, usefulness, and effort expectancy	Trust in CDSS and need for the system	No specified CDSS, responses based on past and present experiences with multiple CDSSs
Sousa et al (2015) [23]	Belief that the suggestions were good for the patient	Low confidence in the evidence	CDSS for nursing care plan
Terraz et al (2005) [24]	Ease of use and easy access to information	Information that is presented is already known	Guidelines for colonoscopies
Wallace et al (1995) [25]	Can improve patient outcomes	Alerts are ignored because there is not enough time to dedicate to forming an appropriate response	CDSS to standardize administration of supplemental oxygen
Zheng et al (2005) [17]	Improves performance leading to better care, easy to use, and efficient	Iterative advisories, lack of relevance, a lot of data entry, and disruptive	Clinical reminders for chronic diseases and preventive care

Figure 4.1 Clinicians have mixed opinions on clinical decision support system. (*Source:* Khairat, S., Marc, D., Crosby, W., and Sanousi, A.A. [2018]. "Reasons for Physicians Not Adopting Clinical Decision Support Systems: Critical Analysis." *JMIR Medical Informatics*, vol. 6, no. 2: e24.⁹ Data derived from https://www.ncbi.nlm.nih.gov/pmc/articles/PMC5932331/?report=printable)

of the alerts they receive, respectively.[10] As stakeholders look for ways to reinvent CDS, they need to be more imaginative in creating and launching alert systems. Among the possible solutions to this overload dilemma:

- Tailor alerts to reach select groups of clinicians based on their role in healthcare. It is less important for hospital-based physicians to know all the details about whether a medication should be taken with milk or other foods, for instance, but far more important for a bedside nurse who is directly administering the drug.
- Provide more precise, personalized alerts that take into account a patient's age, renal and hepatic status, prescribed dosage, and co-existing diseases.
- Give clinicians several alert tiers to choose from, with the most critical alerts in the top tier—which cannot be ignored. It is more important, for instance, for alerts to make clinicians aware of potentially fatal drug interactions than to trigger an alarm about less serious interactions.

Of course, there are alert system success stories worth telling. An analysis of over 26,000 inpatient encounters in the Cedars-Sinai Health System in Los Angeles, California, found that hospital length of stay was 6.2% lower among patients whose clinicians adhered to CDS alerts, when compared to a control group that did not. The total encounter cost was 7.3% higher in patients when their practitioners ignored the recommendations. "Full adherence to Choosing Wisely alerts was associated with savings of $944 from a median encounter cost of $12,940."[11] The alerts were based on guidelines from the Choosing Wisely program, developed by the American Board of Internal Medicine Foundation, the goal of which is to encourage physicians to avoid a long list of medical services that are unwarranted. The health system's CDS program was developed by Optum Inc.

Another obstacle to full acceptance of CDS systems relates back to the Type 1 and Type 2 reasoning modes that clinicians are accustomed to. As we pointed out in Chapter 1, Type 1 diagnostic reasoning relies on quick, intuitive thinking and often uses simple heuristics and cognitive shortcuts. Many clinicians want their CDS system to follow this same fast track way of thinking. Although there is certainly a place for this approach when dealing with routine and easy to recognize disorders, clinicians need to switch to the more deliberate, slower, more analytic Type 2 approach when faced with less obvious diagnostic puzzles. The challenge of getting clinicians to fully embrace CDS systems, then, requires a 2-pronged strategy: CDS systems have to be better designed to allow practitioners to arrive at diagnostic and therapeutic decisions more rapidly through a combination of finely tuned rules and machine learning algorithms. But equally important, practitioners need to be trained to see the importance of slowing down when faced with a complex situation that requires a slow, methodical analysis.

Yet another obstacle that CDS system designers must contend with is clinicians' need to maintain their autonomy during the decision-making process. Khairat et al. sum up the situation this way:

> *If a user finds a product frustrating or perceives that the purpose of the product is to limit autonomy, the user may not use the product or do so inappropriately. . . . [Researchers] . . . explain the consequence of loss of autonomy as reactance. Reactance is an unpleasant motivational state whereby people react to situations to retain freedom and autonomy. Reactance may exist when physicians feel threatened by clinical reminders for fear that they are losing autonomy and freedom of choice in the presence of such systems. Physicians may have the perception that these systems are meant to replace or degrade their clinical duties. [Researchers] . . . describe how unsolicited advice may lead to a reactance state if the advice contradicts a person's original impression of choice options.*[9]

Interviews with physicians, nurses, IT staffs, and boards of directors at 4 British hospitals suggest that their desire to maintain autonomy is a significant barrier to CDS system adoption. Several were also concerned that relying on these expert knowledge systems—or ignoring their advice—may expose them to malpractice claims, should patients develop complications.[12] Liberati et al. summarize the reasoning of clinicians who are not comfortable using CDS systems: "[H]ealth professionals sometimes discard the use of evidence out of fear of compromising their critical reasoning, medical judgments, and professional autonomy or because scientific evidences challenge deep-rooted hierarchies and systems of power based on seniority."

On the subject of malpractice risk, there is some cause for concern because there are case reports in the medical literature documenting adverse reactions caused by CDS systems. An analysis of 47 cases in which CDS systems were linked to adverse effects found that 7 involved CDSS content; the rest were related to how the systems presented their results. A separate study that looked at 79 adverse events that developed within computerized physician order entry systems found 1 out of 4 were related to CDSS.[13] By way of illustration, a case study reported that a 63-year-old patient with an acute myocardial infarction was given carvedilol, an alpha/beta–blocking drug, while in the hospital. During discharge, a resident was advised by a CDSS alert of the need to order a beta-blocking agent in such patients, at which point he prescribed atenolol. Two days later, the patient was in the emergency department experiencing bradycardia and hypotension, the direct result of combining the two drugs. As it turns out, the CDSS had failed to categorize alpha/beta blockers in a way that would overlap with drugs categorized as beta blockers, so the resident ordering atenolol never received the appropriate alert about carvedilol.

Commercially Available CDS Systems

Despite the numerous problems facing CDS systems, many clinicians continue to find them useful, as evidenced by reports from research organizations like KLAS. KLAS interviews 2,500 healthcare professionals each month and taps the opinions of more than 4,500 hospitals and 2,500 clinics, payers, and employer organizations to generate its reports. The 2019 "Best in KLAS Software & Services" report gave its highest rankings to three vendors for their point-of-care CDS tools: UpToDate, from Wolters Kluwer, DynaMed and DynMed Plus from EBSCO Health, and Clinical Key from Elsevier.[14] Similarly, the KLAS report listed Elsevier's Care Planning and ProVation as the 2 best-in-class CDS Care Plans/Order Sets.

Clinicians now have access to a wide array of CDS tools. The following summaries are by no means comprehensive:

DynaMed. DynaMed describes itself as a point-of-care reference tool that includes daily evidence synthesis and objective analysis, with an emphasis on the word "daily." In addition to being used by more than 1 million clinicians worldwide, it is provided on a national scale by several countries, including Scotland, Wales, and Brazil. Several professional associations also make the CDS system available to their members, including the American Medical Association, American College of Physicians, and Canadian Medical Association. DynaMed stands out among CDS vendors because it updates its content more frequently, a claim that is supported by several research reports in the peer-reviewed medical literature. An evaluation of evidence-based point-of-care tools conducted by the medical science library at A & M University concluded that "[six] tools claimed to update summaries within 6 months or less. For the 10 topics searched, however, only DynaMed met this claim."[15]

DynaMed Plus takes a more advanced approach to evidence-based CDS by providing users with a tool it refers to as systematic literature surveillance. Most clinicians realize the value of systematic literature reviews, but these reviews cannot always scale to meet one's informational needs while staying current. DynaMed Plus employs a 7-step methodology that includes systematic search, inclusion criteria, critical appraisal, synthesizing several evidential reports, and daily updating to determine if the search results answer the user's query (Figure 4.2).

Systematic Literature Surveillance
DynaMed 7-Step Methodology

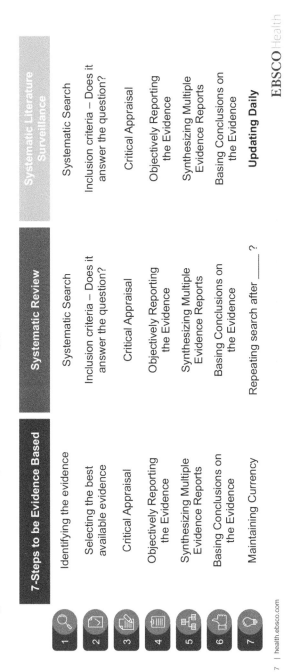

7-Steps to be Evidence Based	Systematic Review	Systematic Literature Surveillance
Identifying the evidence	Systematic Search	Systematic Search
Selecting the best available evidence	Inclusion criteria – Does it answer the question?	Inclusion criteria – Does it answer the question?
Critical Appraisal	Critical Appraisal	Critical Appraisal
Objectively Reporting the Evidence	Objectively Reporting the Evidence	Objectively Reporting the Evidence
Synthesizing Multiple Evidence Reports	Synthesizing Multiple Evidence Reports	Synthesizing Multiple Evidence Reports
Basing Conclusions on the Evidence	Basing Conclusions on the Evidence	Basing Conclusions on the Evidence
Maintaining Currency	Repeating search after ____ ?	**Updating Daily**

Figure 4.2 DynaMed Plus uses a 7-step method, including systematic search, inclusion criteria, critical appraisal, synthesizing several evidential reports, and daily updating to determine if the search results answer the user's query. (Courtesy of EBSCO Health.)

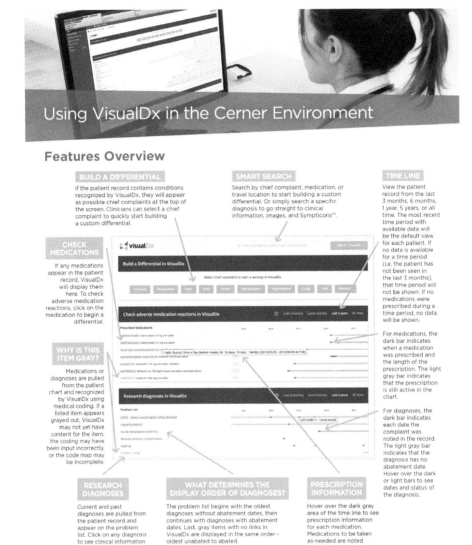

Figure 4.3   An example of how VisualDx can be folded into the Cerner EHR with the help of FHIR protocol. (Graphic provided courtesy of Visual Dx.)

Visual Dx. Clinicians who are more interested in symptom checkers and a differential diagnosis list may prefer Visual Dx's approach to CDS. They can build a differential list by entering a chief complaint, medication, travel history, or other findings into the search boxes. The service excels at pinpointing dermatologic disorders and other disorders with dermatologic features. The search results also include a strength metric to gauge the relevance of the diagnostic suggestions.

For example, starting with a chief compliant of chest pain, the system takes the user to a second page to input the patient's age, gender, general appearance, lab data, X-ray readings, and other markers. If one adds leg pain and increased troponin levels and chooses differential diagnosis, Visual Dx will provide several graphics boxes and list the strengths of the differential diagnoses. The list of likely disorders includes pulmonary embolism and myocardial infarction. Choosing one of the options then takes the user to a detailed discussion of the disorder, including possible atypical presentations, as well as likely EKG readings, CT scans, and X-ray findings. There are also links for each diagnosis to access diagnostic pearls, the best tests to perform to confirm the tentative diagnosis, ICD codes, drug-reaction data, and patient information.

VisuaDX has been embedded into several EHR products, which makes it easier for clinicians to use without disrupting their normal workflow (Figure 4.3). The CDS system is a cloud-based application and uses clustering and auto-scaling. Rolling deployment and session replication allows VisualDx to update content without interrupting the service. It uses SMART on FHIR and the HL7 infobutton to allow integration with a variety of EHR products. Figure 4.3 illustrates how the service has been folded into the Cerner environment, with the help of the FHIR protocol.

ClinicalKey. Elsevier offers several CDS tools, including ClinicalKey, a search engine that lets clinicians find relevant knowledge to help make them make diagnostic and treatment decisions. Like many CDS systems, it can be integrated into an EHR system and accessed from desktop and mobile devices. A search of the term "chest pain," for instance, yields a list of useful citations from leading medical journals on the topic. The search can be refined to pull up RCTs, meta-analyses, guidelines, images, and other specific types of scientific papers. It is also possible to call up articles related to various medical specialties. Elsevier has added ClinicalKey for Nursing to its product set as well.

ClinicalKey is only one type of CDS tool available from the company. It also provides order sets, care planning products, and a cancer care service called ViaOncology. ExpertPath is a CDS system specifically designed to assist pathologists, and ImmunoQuery offers evidence-based support for immunochemistry.

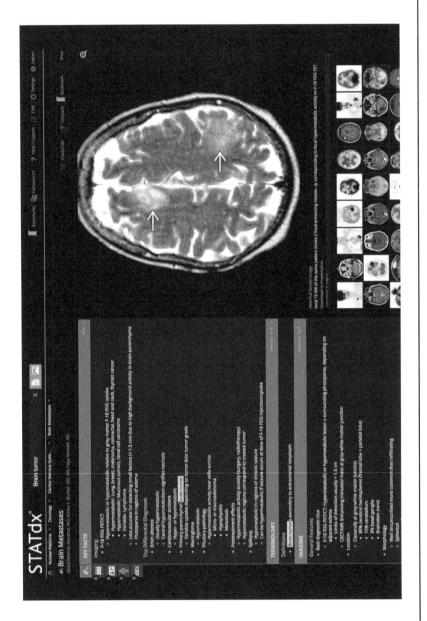

Figure 4.4 STATdx is intended for radiologists, giving them access to 200,000 images, 20,000 patient cases, and 1,300 differential diagnoses modules. (Courtesy of Elsevier.)

Finally, STATdx is intended for radiologists, giving them access to 200,000 images, 20,000 patient cases, and 1,300 differential diagnoses modules. Figure 4.4 is an example of one of the STATdx entries.

UpToDate. This searchable database, from Wolters Kluwer, is widely used by clinicians around the world. The company recently released UpToDate Advanced, which provides a more interactive approach to CDS, offering diagnostic and treatment pathways to help clinicians navigate the complexities of patient care (Figure 4.5). Pathways have been developed for anesthesiology, cardiovascular medicine, hypertension, emergency medicine, endocrinology, gastroenterology, hepatology, infectious disease, primary care, and other specialties. If one chooses the pathway for low back pain, for example, UpToDate initially lists a series of exclusions that are not being considered in the pathway. Nor is pain that persists for more than 4 weeks part of the pathway. The pathway is limited to adults with acute, non-traumatic pain and focuses on spinal pain. The decision tree then takes the reader through a series of Yes/No decision splits to help determine the best course of action, walking us through various diagnostic options and their implications.

Like VisualDx, UpToDate sees an essential role for the FHIR protocol in the future of CDS. In addition to "standalone" use, UpToDate pathways can be integrated with electronic health records (EHRs) using SMART on FHIR technology. When used in integrated mode, answers to many of the questions are prepopulated using data from the EHR, thereby streamlining the experience for the clinician. In addition, both the SMART on FHIR app itself as well as a separate CDS Hooks service can be leveraged to recommend Pathways for a particular patient.

Isabel Healthcare. This CDS system has invested heavily in machine learning. Jason Maude, its CEO and co-founder, points out the limitations of rule-based CDS systems and emphasizes the value of natural language processing and ML to train the tool to learn from clinicians' input (Figure 4.6). As Figure 4.7 illustrates, clinicians input a list of signs and symptoms, as well as travel history, patient age, pregnancy status, and gender and obtain a list of ranked diagnoses.

Several studies published in peer-reviewed journals support the value of Isabel as a diagnostic assistant. Nicholas Riches, with the University of Manchester (Manchester, UK), and his associates conducted a systematic review and meta-analysis of several differential diagnoses (DDX) generators and concluded that as a group they did not improve diagnostic retrieval when compared to what clinicians were capable of on their own, but they also reported that "small improvements were seen in the before and after studies wherein clinicians had

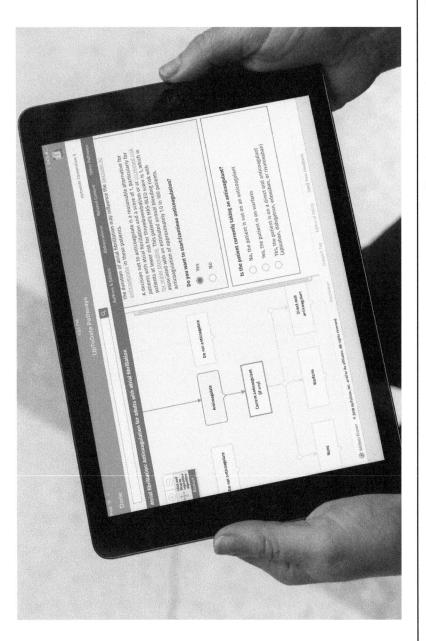

Figure 4.5 UpToDate Advanced, which provides a more interactive approach to CDS, offers diagnostic and treatment pathways to help clinicians navigate the complexities of patient care. (Courtesy of Wolters Kluwer.)

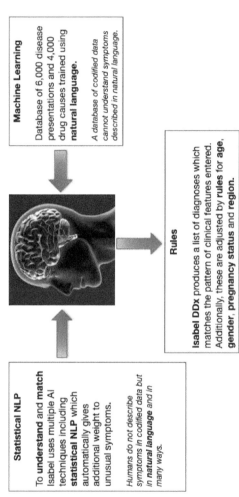

Isabel DDx- Enhanced Machine Learning

Machine Learning

Database of 6,000 disease presentations and 4,000 drug causes trained using **natural language.**

A database of codified data cannot understand symptoms described in natural language.

Statistical NLP

To **understand** and **match** Isabel uses multiple AI techniques including **statistical NLP** which automatically gives additional weight to unusual symptoms.

*Humans do not describe symptoms in codified data but in **natural language** and in many ways.*

Rules

Isabel DDx produces a list of diagnoses which matches the pattern of clinical features entered. Additionally, these are adjusted by **rules** for **age, gender, pregnancy status** and **region.**

Machine learning works out *and* maintains the probabilities

Figure 4.6 Because rule-based CDS systems have their limitations, Isabel Healthcare relies on natural language processing and ML to train the tool to learn from clinicians' input. (Courtesy of Isabel Healthcare.)

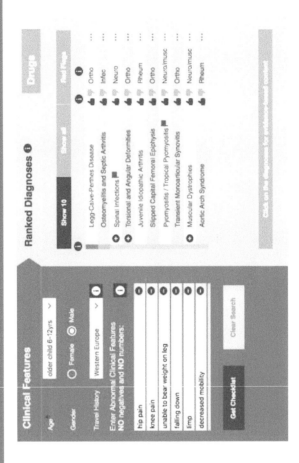

Figure 4.7 The Isabel system lets clinicians input a list of signs and symptoms, as well as travel history, patient age, pregnancy status, and gender and obtain a list of ranked diagnoses. (Courtesy of Isabel Healthcare.)

the opportunity to revisit their diagnoses following DDX generator consultation."[16] On a positive note, Riches et al. also found that "ISABEL was associated with the highest rates of accurate diagnosis retrieval compared to all other types of DDX tools."

Specialized CDS Tools Improve Radiological Reports/Analysis

Previous chapters have highlighted the value of AI in a variety of diagnostic scenarios, including the diagnosing of diabetic retinopathy, breast cancer, and melanoma. But AI is also making progress in the radiology suite itself, offering clinicians tools that move beyond the traditional picture archiving and communication system (PACS). In the past, frontline practitioners would typically receive a plain text document from a radiologist. They would then have to review the images in question in a separate system. One problem with this approach is that it's easy to misinterpret comments in the text report when it is not directly linked to a specific spot on the image in the second application. In practical terms, this means that the referring clinician may think the radiologist is referring to one abnormality on the image when he or she is actually referring to a different problem located elsewhere. Linking the two applications together and adding hyperlinks can significantly improve the quality of the report and the referring physician's ability to interpret the radiology findings.

At the University of Virginia Health System, Cree Gaskin, MD, and his colleagues have devised a hybrid system that includes an AI-enhanced, interactive, multimedia report that takes radiology to a new level, using Vue Reporting and PACS from Carestream Health. Gaskin explains: "Advanced reports support the use of rich content, like styled text, images, tables, graphs and hyperlinks, to improve communication around medical imaging findings. These enhancements can add speed and clarity to report and image review."[17] As Figure 4.8 shows, it is even possible to insert measurements and series numbers in the report that goes to the referring clinician. The hybrid application used by radiologists at the University of Virginia also lets radiologists use voice commands to automatically add these links and measurements to their reports. In Figure 4.8, the right kidney has been highlighted, and, with the help of an AI tool, the relevant measurements are automatically added to the report, overlaid on the exact section of the kidney that the radiologist wants the viewer to see. The hyperlinks added to the images are what make these enhanced reports interactive. When referring clinicians or patients click on the links, it will take them directly to a more detailed view of the radiologist's findings.

Hyperlinks and A.I. Powered Context-Aware Tools

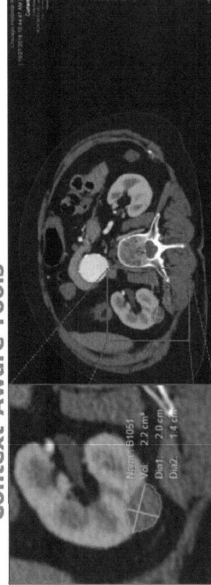

FINDINGS:

[The lung bases are clear. The heart size is normal, without pericardial thickening or effusion.]

[The central pulmonary arteries are without evidence for filling defect to suggest pulmonary embolus or thrombus.]

[The aorta is without aneurysmal dilatation or dissection. Aortic vascular calcifications are present.]

[The liver is normal in size and density without focal mass or intrahepatic biliary dilatation.]

[There is a lesion in the right kidney with a maximum diameter of (2.0 cm) (series 4, image 162).]

[The spleen is normal in size and homogeneous in density.]

Figure 4.8 Using Vue Reporting and PACS from Carestream Health, the University of Virginia Health System can generate advanced reports that support the use of rich content, for example, styled text, images, tables, graphs, and hyperlinks. (Courtesy of Cree Gaskin and Carestream Health.)

Non-Commercial CDS Resources

Implementing the CDS systems described above may require a large budget and a large staff of IT-savvy clinicians and technology specialists. For providers interested in taking a less expensive or labor-intensive approach to CDS, there are a few non-profit organizations available that can provide assistance. The US Department of Health and Human Services, for example, has tasked its Agency for Healthcare Research and Quality (AHRQ) with this mission. AHRQ has launched a CDS-related program, located at https://cds.ahrq.gov, the purpose of which is to show providers how evidence-based patient care can be incorporated into clinical practice. It offers a national repository of CDS resources. Edwin Lomotan, MD, chief of Clinical Informatics and AHRQ, further explains that: "It is the home for the CDS logic that drives the use-case demonstration and is the platform for authoring and sharing the CDS logic."[18]

Healthcare providers interested in developing a CDS tool from the ground up rather than investing in a commercial, prepackaged system typically work through 4 stages in the development process, starting with (1) narrative text derived from a clinical guidelines database; (2) a semi-structured text that explains the recommendations to be implemented in the CDS; (3) structured code that is interpretable by a computer, including data elements, value sets, and logic; and (4) the creation of executable code that can be read by a CDS system locally. To help organizations work through this process, the AHRQ program provides 4 main components:

- The Patient-Centered Clinical Decision Support Learning Network
- CDS Connect, located at https://cds.ahrq.gov/cdsconnect
- An evaluation project
- Funding opportunities

The CDS Connect section includes an authoring tool, as well as a repository that helps users develop high-quality CDS systems. The CDS Authoring Tool provides an interface for creating CDS logic using simple forms and export-ing it as Health Level Seven (HL7) Clinical Quality Language (CQL) artifacts using the HL7 Fast Healthcare Interoperability Resources (FHIR) data model. (A relatively jargon-free explanation of FHIR has been presented by Russell Leftwich from InterSystems and is available online.[19])

Harvard Medical School's Library of Evidence is also a valuable asset for providers interested in developing a robust CDS system. The Library's goal is to "create a provider-led, sustainable, public repository of medical evidence to enable and promote the broad and consistent practice of evidence-based medicine in the United States in order to improve the quality of care while simultaneously reducing waste and cost."[20] The Library is a credible source of guidelines and recommendations on imaging studies. Users who set up an account can gain free access to hundreds of documents and export them in either the FHIR or XML format. The library allows users to search with several filters, including body region, specialty, age group, study design, signs and symptoms, and professional association. It also gives users access to the Choosing Wisely database, which encourages more cost-effective employment of diagnostic testing.

Several US federal agencies provide useful resources to help hospitals and medical practices develop and implement CDS systems. HealthIT.gov, for example, suggests strategies in a report entitled "Optimizing Strategies for Clinical Decision Support." The report was the result of a project spearheaded by the Office of the National Coordinator and the National Academy of Medicine.[21]

CDS Hits a Psychosocial Roadblock

A CDS tool, no matter how sophisticated or reinvented, will only prove effective in improving patient care if patients actually heed the diagnostic and treatment recommendations it generates. And acceptance of that advice does not depend solely on the strength of the scientific evidence supporting the recommendations. In fact, it may have little to do with the evidence—and a great deal to do with the amount of trust that patients have in us as individual practitioners. Over the decades, trust and confidence in the advice of physicians and in evidence-based medicine in general has deteriorates dramatically, as has the public's attitude toward science.

Physicians and nurses who have been trained to think in terms of clinical trials, epidemiological studies, and physiologically plausible mechanisms of action often find it hard to understand the criteria patients use to judge the value of medical interventions. With ready access to the Internet and social media, many have more trust in some online "wellness expert" or the recommendation of a close relative who has never disappointed them before. They may also find it appealing to believe that the "industrial/medical establishment" is only interested in fleecing them of their hard-earned money, convinced that this establishment will invent all sorts of medico-techno babble to confuse and intimidate them. (The fact that even top experts sometimes disagree on the best course of action doesn't help patients trying to figure out who to trust either.)

There was a time when the public had unquestionable faith in biomedicine and the practitioners who translated it into everyday patient care—and physicians believed that the public's trust was justified based on their educational qualifications and training. But today, many patients believe that individual clinicians must *earn* their trust, just as a close relative has earned it through shared experience. Of course, it is exceedingly difficult for busy clinicians to duplicate the bonds developed between relatives, bonds forged through years of laughter and tears.

Richard Baron, MD, from the American Board of Internal Medicine, and Adam Berinsky, PhD, with the Massachusetts Institute of Technology, draw attention to Gallup polling over the last several decades that demonstrates how much the public's confidence in most US institutions has deteriorated. Confidence in the medical system in particular fell from 80% in 1975 to 37% in 2015. Statistics from the General Social Survey confirm this troubling trend.[22] Baron and Berinsky explain the historical reasons for this shift in attitudes, but the more pressing question is: How can individual clinicians, and the profession as a whole, regain patients' trust?

Those of us trained in the scientific method may try to convince skeptical patients to apply what our CDS tools recommend by citing all the facts supporting the recommendations, but there is little reason to believe that this approach works. In the short term, a more psychosocial approach appears to be more effective. At Intermountain Healthcare, for example, one of its ED departments has received higher patient satisfaction scores than its other EDs by using a very simple tactic. As each ED staff member leaves the patient's room, they routinely speak well of the clinicians who are about to enter the room for follow-up care. The patient satisfaction surveys suggest that this small dose of emotional intelligence was enough to elicit trust in the ED staff.

What may work over the long term is developing long-term relationships with patients so that they come to realize that we really do have their best interests at heart—a difficult prescription given today's fragmented healthcare system. Baron and Berinsky state the issue succinctly: "Perhaps the problem with facts is that they stand alone, with no context beyond the scientific method used to generate them. Their 'objective' nature, revered by physicians, is precisely what disconnects them from patients' individual predicaments. . . . If doctors and health care systems are to become more effective in marshaling facts, they will need to become better at giving them meaning by connecting them to individual patients' predicaments, which will require a more intentional effort to create relationships."[22]

References

1. Middleton, B., Sittig, B. F., and Wright, A. (2016). "Clinical Decision Support: A 25 Year Retrospective and a 25 Year Vision." *Yearbook of Medical Informatics,* Aug 2; Suppl 1, S103–116; doi: 10.15265/IYS-2016-s034.

2. Groenhof, T. K., Asselbergs, F. K., Groenwold, R. H. Grobbee, D. E., Visseren, F. L., Bots, M. L.; UCC-SMART Study Group. (2019). "The Effect of Computerized Decision Support Systems on Cardiovascular Risk Factors: A Systematic Review and Meta-Analysis." *BMC Medical Informatics and Decision Making*, vol. 19, p. 108; doi.org/10.1186/s12911-019-0824-x

3. Kawamoto K., Houlihan, C. A., Balas, E. A., and Lobach, D. F. (2005, April 2). "Improving Clinical Practice Using Clinical Decision Support Systems: A Systematic Review of Trials to Identify Features Critical to Success." *BMJ*, vol. 330, no. 7494, p. 765. Epub 2005 Mar 14.

4. Varghese, J., Kleine, M., Gessner, S. I., Sandmann, S., and Dugas, M. (2018). "Effects of Computerized Decision Support System Implementations on Patient Outcomes in Inpatient Care: A Systematic Review." *Journal of American Medical Informatics Association*, vol. 25, pp. 593–602.

5. Blum, D., Raj, S. X., Oberholzer, R., Riphagen, I. I., Strasser, F., and Kaasa, S. (2015). "Computer-Based Clinical Decision Support Systems and Patient-Reported Outcomes: A Systematic Review." *Patient,* vol. 8, pp. 397–409.

6. Ali, S. M., Giordano, R., Lakhani, S., and Walker, D. M. (2016). "A Review of Randomized Controlled Trials of Medical Record Powered Clinical Decision Support System to Improve Quality of Diabetes Care." *International Journal of Medical Informatics,* vol. 87, pp. 91–100.

7. Hussey, P. S., Timbie, J. W., Burgette, L. F., Wenger, N. S., Nyweide, D. J., and Kahn, K. L. (2015). "Appropriateness of Advanced Diagnostic Imaging Ordering Before and After Implementation of Clinical Decision Support Systems." *JAMA,* vol. 313, pp. 2181–2182.

8. Centers for Disease Control and Prevention. (2018, March 22). "Implementing Clinical Decision Support Systems." Retrieved from https://www.cdc.gov/dhdsp/pubs/guides/best-practices/clinical-decision-support.htm

9. Khairat, S., Marc, D., Crosby, W., and Sanousi, A. A. (2018). "Reasons for Physicians Not Adopting Clinical Decision Support Systems: Critical Analysis." *JMIR Medical Informatics,* vol. 6, no. 2: e24.

10. Kesselheim, A. S., Cresswell, K., Phansalkar, S., Bates, D. W., and Sheikh, A. (2011). "Clinical Decision Support Systems Could Be Modified to Reduce 'Alert Fatigue' While Still Minimizing the Risk of Litigation." *Health Affairs,* vol. 30, pp. 2311–2317.

11. Heekin, A. M., Kontor, J., Sax, H. C., Keller, M. S., Wellington, A., and Weingarten, S. (2018). "Choosing Wisely Clinical Decision Support Adherence and Associated Inpatient Outcomes." *American Journal of Managed Care,* vol. 24, pp. 361–366.

12. Liberati, E. G., Ruggiero, F., Galuppo, L., Gorli, M., González-Lorenzo, M., Maraldi, M., and Ruggieri, P. (2017). "What Hinders the Uptake of Computerized Decision Support Systems in Hospitals? A Qualitative Study and Framework for Implementation." *Implementation Science,* vol. 12, p. 113; doi: 10.1186/s13012-017-0644-2

13. Stone, E. G. (2018). "Unintended Adverse Consequences of a Clinical Decision

Support System: Two Cases." *Journal of American Medical Informatics Association,* vol. 25, no. 5, pp. 654–567.

14. KLAS. "Best in KLAS Software & Services 2019." (2019). Retrieved from https://klasresearch.com/report/2019-best-in-klas-software-services/1473

15. Shurtz, S. and Foster, M. J. (2011). "Developing and Using a Rubric for Evaluating Evidence-Based Medicine Point-of-Care Tools." *Journal of Medical Library Association,* vol. 99, pp. 247–254.

16. Riches,N., Panagioti, M., Alam,R., Cheraghi-Sohi, S., Campbell, S., Esmail, A., and Bower P. (2016). "The Effectiveness of Electronic Differential Diagnoses (DDX) Generators: A Systematic Review and Meta-Analysis." *PLOS One,* vol. 11, p. e0148991. Retrieved from https://www.ncbi.nlm.nih.gov/pmc/articles/PMC4782994/

17. Siwicki, B. (2018, Nov 12). "Health System Moves from Text-Only to AI-Powered Interactive Multimedia Radiology Reports." *Healthcare IT News.* Retrieved from https://www.healthcareitnews.com/news/health-system-moves-text-only-ai-powered-interactive-multimedia-radiology-reports

18. Lomotan, E. (2018, March). "Building a Future for Shared Clinical Decision Support." Agency for Healthcare Research and Quality, Rockville, MD. Retrieved from https://www.ahrq.gov/news/blog/ahrqviews/building-a-future-for-shared-cds.html

19. Leftwich, R. (2016, May 26). "The Path to Deriving Clinical Value from FHIR." InterSystems. Retrieved from https://www.youtube.com/watch?v=79aTwUlzRSI#action=share

20. Harvard Medical School Library of Evidence. (2015). "About the Library of Evidence." Retrieved from https://libraryofevidence.med.harvard.edu/about.html#about

21. Tcheng, J. E., Bakken, S., Bates, D. W., Bonner, H., Gandhi, T. K., and Josephs, M. (2017). "Optimizing Strategies for Clinical Decision Support." National Academy of Medicine. Retrieved from https://www.healthit.gov/sites/default/files/page/2018-04/Optimizing_Strategies_508.pdf

22. Baron, R. J. and Berinsky, A. J. (2019). "Mistrust in Science—A Threat to the Patient-Physician Relationship." *New England Journal of Medicine,* vol. 381, pp. 182–185.

Chapter 5

Reengineering Data Analytics

Not everything that can be counted counts, and not everything that counts can be counted.
— William Bruce Cameron[*]

Clinicians in community practice may find it difficult to see the relevance of convolutional neural networks, random forest modeling, clustering, support vector machines, and other esoteric artificial intelligence (AI) tools to their everyday responsibilities. They are certainly not the only ones who remain skeptical. Many medical researchers who have spent years designing and conducting clinical trials may also have a hard time seeing the value of these emerging AI and machine learning (ML) methods for determining the most effective diagnostic and therapeutic options. Despite their doubts, a closer look at several recent analyses demonstrates that big data and all the related analytical tools are affecting the way we interpret clinical research and its impact on direct patient care. Several reports published in the peer-reviewed medical literature illustrate the changing paradigm.

The Future of Subgroup Analysis

Many clinical studies that compare one or more interventions typically generate a mean result and a variance around that average. Over the years, investigators

---

[*] Marconi, K. and Lehmann, H. (2015). *Big Data and Health Analytics* (p. 212). Boca Raton (FL): CRC Press/Taylor & Francis Group.

have used a variety of statistical methods to measure that variance, including the standard deviation, forest plots, and subgroup analysis. But the emergence of several AI/ML–enabled techniques suggests that these older approaches are insufficient because they do not always detect the heterogeneity present in patient populations.

A case in point is the Look AHEAD study published in 2013.[1] This large-scale randomized controlled trial (RCT) assigned over 5,000 overweight and obese patients with type 2 diabetes to either an intensive lifestyle modification program or to a control group that only received supportive education. The investigators' goal was to determine if the lifestyle program would reduce the incidence of death from cardiovascular disease, non-fatal myocardial infarction, non-fatal stroke, or hospitalization for angina. The original plan was to follow these patients for as long as 13.5 years but the study was terminated early because there were no significant differences between the intervention and control groups. The lower caloric content and increased exercise in the intensive lifestyle group did have a positive impact, helping patients to lose weight, but it did not reduce the rate of cardiovascular events.

The Look AHEAD researchers performed a subgroup analysis to see if certain portions of the patient population may have experienced better clinical outcomes. They looked more closely at patients by gender, race, or ethnic group, and the presence or absence of cardiovascular disease when they enrolled in the study. A forest plot analysis found no significant differences.

Aaron Baum and his colleagues at Icahn School of Medicine at Mount Sinai, New York, and elsewhere were not satisfied with those results and decided to do a much more in-depth subgroup analysis.[2] They used an advanced ML method called random forest modeling. One advantage of this method is that it does not start with a specific hypothesis on what variables or patient population characteristics may be responsible for possible heterogenous treatment effects. The original research project, on the other hand, hypothesized that a patient's gender, ethnicity, or history of cardiovascular disease may have influenced their response to treatment. During random forest analysis, a series of decision trees are created—thus the term "forest." Initially, the technique randomly splits all the available data—in this case, the stored characteristics of about 5,000 patients in the Look AHEAD study—into two halves. The first half serves as a training data set to generate hypotheses and construct the decision trees. The second half of the data serves as the testing data set. As Baum et al. explain, "The method first identifies subgroups with similar treatment effects in the training data, then tests the most promising heterogeneous treatment effect (HTE) hypotheses on the testing data . . ."[2]

Using this technique, Baum et al. constructed a forest that contained 1,000 decision trees and looked at 84 co-variates that may have been influencing patients' response or lack of response to the intensive lifestyle modification program. These variables included a family history of diabetes, muscle cramps in legs and feet, a history of emphysema, kidney disease, amputation, dry skin, loud snoring, marital status, social functioning, hemoglobin A1c, self-reported health, and numerous other characteristics that researchers rarely if ever consider when doing a subgroup analysis. The random forest analysis also allowed the investigators to look at how numerous variables *interact* in multiple combinations to impact clinical outcomes. The Look AHEAD subgroup analyses looked at only 3 possible variables and only one at a time.

In the final analysis, Baum et al. discovered that intensive lifestyle modification averted cardiovascular events for two subgroups, patients with HbA1c 6.8% or higher (poorly managed diabetes) and patients with well-controlled diabetes (Hba1c < 6.8%) and good self-reported health. That finding applied to 85% of the entire patient population studied. On the other hand, the remaining 15% who had controlled diabetes but poor self-reported general health responded negatively to the lifestyle modification regimen. The negative and positive responders cancelled each other out in the initial statistical analysis, falsely concluding that lifestyle modification was useless. The Baum et al. reanalysis lends further support to the belief that a one-size-fits-all approach to medicine is inadequate to address all the individualistic responses that patients have to treatment.[2]

Scarpa et al. likewise provide support for a more personalized approach to patient care. They also used random forest analysis, in this case to assess the heterogenous effects of intensive blood pressure reduction in patients with hypertension.[3] They reanalyzed the results of the Systematic Blood Pressure Intervention Trial (SPRINT), which found that lowering systolic BP to below 120 mm Hg in patients without diabetes was more effective than setting a more modest target of less than 140 mm Hg. Specifically, SPRINT found that the intensive program reduced the incidence of myocardial infarction, other acute coronary syndromes, stroke, heart failure, or death from other cardiovascular diseases.[4] Scarpa et al. evaluated data from over 9,000 patients enrolled in SPRINT, which included 466 who were smokers and had systolic BP above 144 mm Hg. They divided this latter subgroup in half, with 236 patients randomized to a training data set and 236 to a testing data set. They then looked at the combination of 2 co-variates, namely, smoking status and systolic BP, to see if they may affect study participants differently from the rest of the patient population. It turns out this subgroup did in fact respond differently to intensive BP reduction. Scarpa et al. found that "current smokers with a baseline systolic blood pressure greater than 144 mm Hg had a higher rate of cardiovascular events in the intensive treatment group vs the standard treatment group." These smokers were also more likely to develop acute kidney injuries on the intensive program when compared to smokers adhering to the more modest BP target (10% vs 3.2%), providing further evidence that one-size-fits all medicine needs to be replaced by a more precise approach that takes into account heterogenous reactions to treatment.[3]

In Chapter 2, we discussed the work of Jeremy Sussman, MD, and his colleagues, who further demonstrated the importance of subgroup analysis to help personalize treatment.[5] Sussman et al. reanalyzed raw data from the landmark Diabetes Prevention Program (DPP), which compared a lifestyle modification program and metformin to placebo in subjects who did not have type 2 diabetes but who were at risk because of three underlying risk factors. They were overweight, had elevated fasting blood glucose readings, and abnormal glucose tolerance tests.[6] The ultimate goal was to determine if either of the 2 experimental treatments would prevent the disease. DPP researchers found that metformin reduced the incidence of diabetes by 31% and lifestyle modification by 58%, when compared to controls. Sussman et al. reanalyzed the original data using proportional hazards regression, which revealed that there were 7 risk factors that would help detect a person's risk of the disease, not the original 3 used in the DPP trial. More importantly, those 7 variables helped to pinpoint individuals more likely to develop diabetes. Those 7 risk factors included fasting blood glucose, HbA1c, family history of elevated blood glucose, blood triglycerides, waist measurement, height, and waist-to-hip ratio.

Using these 7 variables, the reanalysis also revealed that the benefits of metformin were very unevenly distributed in the study population, "with the quarter of patients at the highest risk for developing diabetes receiving a dramatic benefit (21.5% absolute reduction in diabetes over three years of treatment) but the remainder of the study population receiving modest or no benefit."[5]

Clinical guidelines are another area in which one-size-fits-all medicine plays an outsize role in patient care. Perhaps one-size-fits-too-many medicine would be a better term for this overreach. For example, the US Preventive Services Task Force recommends that between age 50 and 75, adults at average risk should be screened for colorectal cancer. Although that narrows down the population requiring screening to a subgroup of Americans, it's a very large subgroup. Recent developments in data analytics suggest it may be possible to make screening recommendations more precise and personalized.

Currently, the guidelines for colorectal cancer screening are based on a person's family history of the disease, but do not take into account all the other relevant risk factors, including lifestyle and environmental and genetic factors. An analysis of more than 9,700 cases of colorectal cancer and more than 10,000 controls has developed a more nuanced approach to risk assessment. Jihyoun Jeon, PhD, with the department of epidemiology at the University of Michigan, Ann Arbor, and his colleagues used patient data from these 2 groups to develop E-scores, which take into account numerous environmental factors, and a G-score to measure genetic predisposition to the cancer. The analysis concluded that the risk of the disease can vary by as much as 12 years for men with the highest risk compared to those with the lowest (10%) risk. For women, there was a 14-year spread.[7]

How did the researchers arrive at their more personalized risk estimates? With the help of ML, they divided the population into two halves, with the first half used to create a risk determination model and the second half to be analyzed to see how accurate the model was in predicting the risk of cancer. The E-score they created took into account 19 metrics, including height, body mass index, educational level, history of type 2 diabetes, alcohol intake, aspirin use, smoking, intake of fiber, calcium, and other nutrients. The G-score factored 63 single nucleotide polymorphisms related to colorectal cancer into their risk analysis. To evaluate the accuracy of the model, Jeon et al. used multivariate logistic regression and area under the curve (AUC). The conclusion: "For those with high-risk of CRC as determined by a positive family history and 90th percentile of the combined risk score of E-score and G-score, the recommended age to start screening is 40 for men and 46 for women, respectively. On the other hand, for those with a positive family history but in the 10th percentile of the combined risk score, the recommended age to begin in men is 51 and in women 59 (i.e., 11 years later for men and 13 years later for women)."[7]

Predicting MS and Emergency Response

Analyzing big data sets also offers insights into a variety of other diseases, including multiple sclerosis (MS). Like colorectal cancer and many other disorders, MS is best managed if it can be detected early on. With that in mind, several attempts have been made to establish an MS prodrome—a set of signs, symptoms and other markers to signal the early onset of the disorder. Tanja Hogg, with the Department of Statistics at the University of British Columbia, in Vancouver, and her colleagues analyzed over 8,000 MS cases and over 40,000 controls to look for markers that suggest the preclinical onset of MS. With the help of logistic regression and penalized logistic regression, they looked at physician and hospital encounters with patients during the 5 years prior to the full onset of MS, which was identified as the first demyelinating event. The encounters were documented as International Classification of Disease (ICD) codes and prescription fills. Hogg et al. found that the physician-derived data accurately predicted which patients would develop full-blown MS, suggesting that patients with diagnoses of central nervous and peripheral diseases, as well as eye and cerebrovascular diseases were the signposts to indicate that MS was down the road. Hospital and drug data, on the other hand, had poor predictive ability.[8] Put another way, "A physician encounter for a cerebrovascular, central or peripheral nervous system-related disease or disorder of the sense organs was associated with 2- to 5-fold higher odds of MS. Findings suggest that an earlier recognition and diagnosis of MS is possible."[8]

Disease prediction is only one of many potential roles for data analytics. It is also being used to glean insights from telehealth programs, including the personal emergency response systems (PERS) that have become popular in the elderly community. The famous ad in which an older adult pleads: "Help I've fallen and I can't get up" has generated an entire industry of PERS bracelets and necklaces that give patients quick access to emergency services with the press of a button. Dutch and American researchers have analyzed medical alert pattern data from almost 300,000 subscribers to a PERS service, using a type of ML called gradient tree boosting. Their predictive model included demographics, medical conditions, and the availability of caregivers in the subscriber's network, along with up to 2 years of retrospective medical alert data.[9]

Among the 289,426 patients in the data set, 2.2% had 12 or more emergency transports in a month; the predictive model was able to stratify patients into low- and high-risk groups. Among the top 1% of patients in the high-risk group, 25.5% had 1 or more trips to the emergency department (ED) in the next 30 days. Analysis of the electronic health record (EHR) data was also revealing: "Clinical observations from the EHR showed that predicted high-risk patients had nearly four times higher rates of emergency encounters than did low-risk patients."[9] Armed with these kinds of statistics, clinicians could offer more targeted preventive care to those at highest risk.

Big Data Meets Medication Management

Data analytics is making progress in the battle to reduce the risk of adverse reactions to medication as well. It is estimated that about 1.5 million preventable adverse drug reactions occur in the United States annually. Among pediatric patients, the rate of adverse drug reactions is about 3 times that seen in adults. And ICU patients face an even more threatening scenario, for several reasons. Since they are often sedated, they cannot report reactions as readily, and they are also more likely to receive drugs by parenteral route. With these concerns in mind, clinical informatics specialists teamed up with physicians, nurses, and pharmacists at Phoenix Children's Hospital to create an enhanced, customized drug range checking (DRC) system, which started with a data analysis project that retrospectively evaluated over 750,000 prescription orders over 8 years.[10]

Unlike the previous DRC system being used at Phoenix—an Allscripts program that only included soft alerts—the enhanced DRC system included both soft and hard alerts. The new system required clinicians to take a "time out" if they wanted to order a medication associated with a soft alert, at which point the prescriber was told the degree to which they exceeded the normal dosage. They then had to acknowledge the alert with a comment. An email was also generated when this occurred and sent to the clinical pharmacist. On the other hand, if a clinician decided they wanted to order a dosage much farther outside standard protocols, a hard stop was issued by the software, at which point they could not order the medication without discussing the decision with an attending physician and a pharmacist.[10]

One of the chief complaints voiced by clinicians who deal with alerts is that they cause alert fatigue, overwhelming them with needless interruptions. The enhanced DRC system addressed this concern: If a clinician received a soft stop, they were allowed to reorder the same dosage for the same patient for the next 72 hours without seeing another alert.[10]

The investigation compared outcomes before and after the new dosage checking systems were installed. They found that with the enhanced program, clinicians reduced dosages to more appropriate levels in about 25% of orders placed, compared to 10% before the system was installed. Similarly, after the enhanced system went live, clinicians deleted 9.5% of their initial medication orders, compared to no cancelled orders before it was installed.[10]

The Role of Data Analytics in Cancer Risk Assessment

In Chapter 2, we discussed the emerging role of AI in evaluating the risk of breast cancer and diagnosing breast cancer nodal metastasis. There is also evidence to demonstrate that big data can be valuable in patients found to have certain genetic variants of BRCA1 and BRCA2, both of which have been shown to greatly increase the risk of breast and ovarian cancer.[11] Patients may incorrectly assume that if they have any mutation in these genes, they are automatically at risk for the cancers, but many of these mutations are benign. The challenge for oncologists and geneticists trying to analyze the results of these tests and give patients accurate advice about the threat of cancer is that it is not always possible to definitively state that a specific genetic variant is benign or malignant. That's the case because there are still many mutations that fall into the category called variants of uncertain clinical significance (VUS); these VUSs account for about 3% of test results, and geneticists estimate that 15% to 20% of this subgroup will likely be found to be pathogenic when enough data is available.

A new database has recently been developed to collect all available information on BRCA1 and BRCA2 variants, which should help clinicians make a more informed decision when interpreting the genetic test. This big data project, which was spearheaded by the Global Alliance for Genomics and Health, has collected data from a variety of sources to create the BRCA Exchange, a "one stop shop" that gleans data from clinicians, clinical labs, and researchers from around the world, combining databases such as ClinVar, Breast Cancer Information Core, and Leiden Open Variation Database. It includes over 20,000 BRCA1 and BRCA2 variants; 6,100 variants have been categorized, with 3,700 considered pathogenic. Clinicians and patients can benefit from this massive database in at least 3 ways. If a search reveals a pathogenic variant of either BRAC gene, they may opt for removal of the patient's breast or ovaries. As an alternative, they may start targeted therapy if a malignancy already exists. And lastly, there's the option of "periodically reappraising patients with variants of uncertain clinical significance."[11]

Susan Domchek, MD, Director of the Basser Center for BRCA at Penn Medicine in Philadelphia, does not encourage patients to take any drastic action based on a VUS finding, being fully aware that fear can result in some patients overreacting to the news. One of the missions of the BRCA Exchange is to collect new data on BRCA variants, their prevalence in the population, their biological effects, and any phenotypic features of diseases that may be linked to the mutations. Domchek warns that clinicians need to be cautious about not jumping to any conclusions about VUS findings, especially in minorities who are underrepresented in the database. They may have "have a different spectrum of what is 'normal' in genetics."

Impact of Data Analytics on Healthcare Costs

Although data analytics and ML will play an important role in clinical medicine over the next several years, there is also evidence to show it is already having an impact on the financial side of medicine. Among the most significant initiatives that are having an effect on healthcare expenditure is the Choosing Wisely program that was launched by several national organizations in 2012 to limit the number of unnecessary tests and procedures performed on patients.[12] The list of questionable tests and procedures is quite long, including routine cholecystectomy for patients with asymptomatic cholelithiasis; routine use of ultrasound in evaluating clinically apparent inguinal hernia; and screening for genital herpes simplex virus infection in asymptomatic adults, including pregnant women.

An analysis of more than 26,000 patient encounters conducted by investigators at Optum and associates from Cedars-Sinai Medical Center and Stanson Health in Los Angeles (CA) compared providers who followed the Choosing Wisely recommendations in the clinical decision support (CDS) system to those who did not. The cost of a patient encounter was 7.3% greater among those who ignored the advice coming from their CDS system. Similarly, length of hospital stay was 6.2% longer among noncompliant practitioners, and the odds ratio of 30-day readmission and complications were greater in this group.[12] Among the data points analyzed: whether the provider was a resident or attending physician, patient demographics, their clinical outcomes, Medicare status, and diagnosis. The final financial analysis concluded: "Full adherence to Choosing Wisely alerts was associated with savings of $944 from a median encounter cost of $12,940."

William Bruce Cameron may have been correct in pointing out that not everything that can be counted actually matters, but the research described above suggests that doing the right kind of counting does in fact have a very real impact on patient care.

References

1. The Look AHEAD Research Group. (2013). "Cardiovascular Effects of Intensive Lifestyle Intervention in Type 2 diabetes." *New England Journal of Medicine,* vol. 369, pp. 145–154.
2. Baum, A., Scarpa, J., Bruzelius, E., Tamler, R., Basu, S., and Faghmous, J. (2017). "Targeting Weight Loss Interventions to Reduce Cardiovascular Complications of Type 2 Diabetes: A Machine Learning-Based Post-Hoc Analysis of Heterogeneous Treatment Effects in the Look AHEAD Trial." *Lancet Diabetes 7 Endocrinology,* vol. 5, pp. 808–815.
3. Scarpa, J., Bruzelius, E., Doupe, P., Le, M., Faghmous, J., and Baum, A. (2019). "Assessment of Risk of Harm Associated with Intensive Blood Pressure Management Among Patients with Hypertension Who Smoke: A Secondary Analysis of the Systolic Blood Pressure Intervention Trial." *JAMA Open,* vol. 2, p. e190005.
4. The SPRINT Research Group. (2015). "A Randomized Trial of Intensive versus Standard Blood-Pressure Control." *New England Journal of Medicine,* vol. 373, pp. 2103–2116.
5. Sussman, J., Kent, D. M., Nelson, J. P., and Hayward R. A. (2015). "Improving Diabetes Prevention with Benefit Based Tailored Treatment: Risk Based Reanalysis of Diabetes Prevention Program." *BMJ,* vol. 350, p. h454.
6. Diabetes Prevention Program Research Group. (2002). "Reduction in the Incidence of Type 2 Diabetes with Lifestyle Intervention or Metformin." *New England Journal of Medicine,* vol. 346, pp. 393–403.

7. Jeon, J., Du, M., Schoen, R. E., Hoffmeister, M., Newcomb, P. A., Berndt, S., Caan, B., and Campbell, P. T. (2018). "Determining Risk of Colorectal Cancer and Starting Age of Screening Based on Lifestyle, Environmental, and Genetic Factors." *Gastroenterology,* vol. 154, pp. 2152–2164.

8. Högg, T., Wijnands, J. M., Kingwell, E., Zhu, F., Lu, X., Evans, C., Fisk, J. D., Marrie, R. A., Zhao, Y., and Tremlett, H. (2018). "Mining Healthcare Data for Markers of the Multiple Sclerosis Prodrome." *Multiple Sclerosis and Related Disorders,* vol. 25, pp. 232–240.

9. Op den Buijs, J., Simons, M., Golas, S., Fischer, N., Felsted, J., Schertzer, L., Agboola, S., Kvedar, J., and Jethwani, K. (2018). "Predictive Modeling of 30-Day Emergency Hospital Transport of Patients Using a Personal Emergency Response System: Prognostic Retrospective Study." *JMIR Medical Informatics,* vol. 6, p. e49.

10. Balasuriya, L., Vyles, D., Bakerman, P., Holton, V., Vaidya, V., Garcia-Filion, P., Westdorp, J., Sanchez, C., and Kurz, R. (2017). "Computerized Dose Range Checking Using Hard and Soft Stop Alerts Reduces Prescribing Errors in a Pediatric Intensive Care Unit." *Journal of Patient Safety,* vol. 13, pp. 144–148.

11. Voelker, R. (2019). "Quick Uptakes: Taking the Uncertainty Out of Interpreting BRCA Variants." *JAMA,* vol. 321, pp. 1340–1341.

12. Heekin, A. M., Kontor, J., Sax, H. C., Keller, M. S., Wellington, A., and Weingarten, S. (2018). "Choosing Wisely Clinical Decision Support Adherence and Associated Inpatient Outcomes." *American Journal of Managed Care,* vol. 24, pp. 361–366.

Chapter 6

Will Systems Biology Transform Clinical Decision Support?

In previous chapters, we discussed the value of clinical decision support (CDS) systems that incorporate artificial intelligence (AI) and machine learning (ML). Although these digital tools can improve the diagnostic process and offer clinicians a variety of state-of-the-art treatment options, most are based on a reductionistic approach to health and disease. This paradigm takes a divide-and-conquer approach to medicine, "rooted in the assumption that complex problems are solvable by dividing them into smaller, simpler, and thus more tractable units."[1] Although this methodology has led to important insights and practical implications in healthcare, it does have its limitations.

Reductionistic thinking has led researchers and clinicians to search for one or two primary causes of each disease and design therapies that address those causes. When HIV was found to be a root cause of AIDS, for instance, virtually all efforts then focused on developing a way to suppress or eliminate the virus. Similarly, the focus of diabetes management is primarily on getting blood glucose levels under control, and a diagnosis of hypothyroidism typically focuses on hormone replacement. The limitation to this type of reasoning becomes obvious when one examines the impact of each of these diseases. There are many individuals who are exposed to HIV who do not develop the infection, many patients have blood glucose levels outside the normal range who never develop signs and symptoms of diabetes, and many patients with low thyroxine

Characteristic	Reductionism	Systems-Oriented Approach
Principle	Behavior of a biological system can be explained by the properties of its constituent parts	Biological systems possess emergent properties that are only possessed by the system as a whole and not by any isolated part of the system
Metaphor	Machine, magic bullet	Network
Approach	One factor is singled out for attention and is given explanatory weight on its own	Many factors are simultaneously evaluated to assess the dynamics of the system
Critical factors	Predictors/associated factors	Time, space, context
Model characteristics	Linear, predictable, frequently deterministic	Non-linear, sensitive to initial conditions, stochastic (probabilistic), chaotic
Medical concepts	Health is normalcy	Health is robustness
	Health is risk reduction	Health is adaptation/plasticity
	Health is homeostasis	Health is homeodynamics

DOI: 10.1371/journal.pmed.0030208.t001

Figure 6.1 Reductionism and systems biology take very different approaches to health and disease. (*Source*: Ahn, A. C., Tewari, M., Poon, C. S., and Phillips, R. S. [2006]. "The Limits of Reductionism in Medicine: Could Systems Biology Offer an Alternative?" *PLOS Medicine*, vol. 3, p. e201.')

levels do not develop clinical hypothyroidism. These "anomalies" imply that there are cofactors involved in all these conditions, which when combined with the primary cause or causes bring about the clinical onset. Detecting these contributing factors requires the reductionist approach to be complemented by a systems biology approach, which assumes that there are many interacting causes to each disease (Figure 6.1).

Redefining Health and Disease

Since the 19th century, medicine has focused on specific disease states by linking collections of signs and symptoms to single organs. Joseph Loscalzo, MD, Harvard Medical School, and his colleagues point out that "this organ-based focus of disease also has served as the driving principle underlying basic research into disease pathogenesis at the physiological, biochemical, and molecular levels."[2] Systems biology and its offspring, sometimes called Network Medicine, takes a more wholistic approach, looking at all the diverse genetic, metabolic, and environmental factors that contribute to clinical disease. Equally important, it looks at the preclinical manifestations of pathology.

The current focus of medicine is much like the focus that an auto mechanic takes to repair a car. The diagnostic process isolates a broken part and repairs or replaces it. Similarly, when a clinician detects an infection, they isolate a specific pathogen and attack it with antibiotics or antiviral agents. If cancer is diagnosed, the tumor becomes the target to be destroyed. If gastrointestinal bleeding is detected, we try to locate the source and stop the bleeding.[1] Although this strategy has saved countless lives and reduced pain and suffering, it nevertheless treats the disease and not the patient, with all their unique habits, lifestyle mistakes, environmental exposures, psychosocial interactions, and genetic predispositions.

The traditional approach to many physiological or biochemical imbalances based on the reductionistic model has its shortcomings. Correcting a low serum potassium, for instance, by administering the electrolyte does not necessarily address the underlying pathology causing the drop in potassium levels. Similarly, administering estrogen therapy to postmenopausal women might seem like a good idea based on the current disease model, but several large-scale clinical trials have demonstrated that estrogen therapy in this context does more harm than good for many older women. The management of hypertension poses another dilemma for the one-size-fits-all mentality behind reductionism. For instance, the Joint National Committee on Prevention, Detection, Evaluation, and Treatment of High Blood Pressure continues to lower its systolic and diastolic blood pressure recommendations for the general public, which leads to many patients being told to lower their readings despite the fact that they do not have heart disease and never will. A more wholistic systems approach would dictate a multidimensional risk assessment that individualizes recommendations. The limitations of the reductionist approach to hypertension management were well illustrated in the reanalysis of the SPRINT study that we discussed in Chapter 5. Scarpa et al. demonstrated that setting a systolic blood pressure target of less than 120 mm Hg may be good advice for patients who did not smoke but has done more harm than good for those who do.[3]

Andrew Ahn, also with Harvard Medical School, and his colleagues discuss the shortcomings of reductionism and the application of systems biology to clinical medicine by explaining:

> In reductionism, multiple problems in a system are typically tackled piecemeal. Each problem is partitioned and addressed individually. In coronary artery disease, for example, each known risk factor is addressed individually, whether it be hyperlipidemia or hypertension. The strategy is also extended to coexisting diseases, such as hypothyroidism, diabetes, and coronary artery disease. Each disease is treated individually, as if the treatment of one disorder (such as coronary artery disease) has minimal effects on the treatment of another (such as hypothyroidism). While this approach is easily executable in clinical practice, it neglects the complex interplay between disease and treatment. The assumption is that the results of treatments are additive rather than nonlinear.[1]

Approaching Diabetes within a Systems Perspective

Factor	Systems-Oriented Practice
Time	Assessing temporal variability of insulin or glucose as a means to predict or diagnose diabetes
	Administering insulin at critical time junctures (aside from pre-meal/pre-sleep times)
	Assessing spatial distribution of insulin or glucose as a means to predict or diagnose diabetes
Space	Administering insulin at sites with optimal effect
Context	Using multiple parameters to determine the type of diabetes (beyond types 1 and 2) affecting the patient
	Administering individualized, sometimes unintuitive treatments (e.g., salicylates for certain individuals)

DOI: 10.1371/journal.pmed.0030209.t002

Figure 6.2 A deeper understanding of how physiological and molecular systems interact to produce health and disease requires that we understand 3 factors that influence the behavior of systems: context, time, and space. (*Source:* Ahn, A. C., Tewari, M., Poon, C. S., and Phillips, R. S. [2006]. "The Clinical Applications of a Systems Approach." *PLOS Medicine*, vol. 3, p. e209.[4])

On the other hand, a deeper understanding of how physiological and molecular systems interact to produce health and disease requires that we understand 3 factors that influence the behavior of systems: context, time, and space (Figure 6.2). We discussed context above, in reference to the unique habits, lifestyle mistakes, environmental exposures, psychosocial interactions, and genetic predispositions. Systems biology researchers have also demonstrated that the concentrations of essential enzymes and other proteins are in a state of constant change, making any static measurement of less value than assessment of these parameters over time, taking into account circadian rhythms and external stressors. Finally, all these physical interactions occur between components in a given space.

How can these insights apply to clinical medicine? The systems biology paradigm seems to be better suited to the management of chronic, complex diseases, as opposed to acute, simple disorders. Acute appendicitis, for instance, has an immediately curable pathology. Removal of the organ usually solves the problem, with no further need for long-term therapy. On the other hand, disorders such as diabetes, coronary artery disease, and asthma will likely respond better to the in-depth analysis and comprehensive data gathering that are characteristic of network medicine (Figure 6.3). As Ahn et al.[1] point out, diabetes is a multidimensional disease involving genetic mutations, inflammation, leptin, cortisol, diet, body mass index, and a host of other contributing factors that all need attention. From that perspective, AI-enabled tools such as IDx-DR and DreaMed Advisor Pro are *cheats*. As discussed in Chapter 2, IDx-DR helps diagnose

Application of Reductionism versus Systems-Oriented Perspective to Medicine

Characteristics	Reductionism	Systems-Oriented Perspective
Optimal	Conditions where one or few components are responsible for the overall behavior of the system	Conditions where interactions between components are responsible for the overall behavior of the system
Disease types	Acute, simple diseases	Chronic, complex diseases
Examples	Urinary tract infection	Diabetes
	Appendicitis	Coronary artery disease
	Aortic aneurysm	Asthma
Theoretical limitations	Disregards component–component interactions and dynamics	Costly in resources and time

DOI: 10.1371/journal.pmed.0030209.t001

Figure 6.3 The systems biology paradigm seems to be better suited to the management of chronic, complex diseases, as opposed to acute, simple disorders. (*Source:* Ahn, A. C., Tewari, M., Poon, C. S., and Phillips, R. S. [2006]. "The Clinical Applications of a Systems Approach." *PLOS Medicine*, vol. 3, p. e209.[4])

diabetic retinopathy, and Advisor Pro helps clinicians better manage blood glucose levels. But since diabetes is much more than abnormal glucose metabolism, these digital tools do not even take us halfway to full disease management.

In the case of diabetes, the diagnosis is currently made when fasting blood glucose levels or a glucose tolerance test reaches a specific threshold. But a systems biology approach suggests that we look instead at the dynamic nature of glucose metabolism over time. One option is to measure blood glucose variability or changes in insulin levels over time, taking into account the fact that in normal individuals, pulsatile secretion of the hormone occurs in 6- to 10-minute oscillations. Patients with Type 2 diabetes, on the other hand, have impaired oscillations. First-degree relatives of patients with Type 2 disease also have impaired pulsatile insulin levels, even before their glucose metabolism becomes abnormal. O'Rahilly et al. performed a time series analysis of fasting plasma insulin in 10 relatives who were only slightly glucose intolerant and compared their readings with 10 healthy controls and found that relatives lacked the regular fluctuations in insulin levels, when compared to normal subjects.[5] Their results suggest that impaired pulsatile insulin may predict the early onset of diabetes. The experiment also emphasizes the value of analyzing the dynamic nature of disease rather than making diagnostic judgments based on cross-sectional snapshots.

Andrew Ahn and his colleagues express this important insight succinctly:

> *Because glucose levels are continually regulated through a dynamic balance between glucose-lowering factors (such as insulin) and glucose-elevating factors (such as glucagons, growth hormone, or epinephrine), the manner in which glucose varies over time may reflect the functional health of the relevant metabolic pathways. The premise is that glucose regulatory pathways are inextricably interconnected and that any dysfunction in the pathway is reflected in the glucose/insulin dynamics. The temporal changes of a variable contain hidden, useful information about the overall system.[4]*

Is Systems Biology Ready for Prime Time Medicine?

Although the concepts and research supporting a systems biology approach to medicine are sound, critics will no doubt question whether they can be applied in patient care as it's currently practiced. ML once again offers promise in converting theory into practice. In previous chapters, we discussed a form of ML called the convolutional neural network, a form of supervised deep learning. In supervised learning, an algorithm analyzes specific data points—for example, a patient's demographics and their risk factors for skin cancer. And then the software looks for links between these data elements and an outcome like melanoma. In technology parlance, this is referred to as labeled ML. Unsupervised learning, on the other hand, does not analyze labeled data elements but goes on a "fishing expedition" to find unexpected relationships, looking at unlabeled or unclassified data, hoping to find hidden relationships and, perhaps, cause-and-effect relationships.

Clustering is one example of unsupervised ML. It seeks to identify groupings within the data and similarities within the data that suggest subsections and patterns. This approach may reveal patient subgroups in an ICU, for instance, who have very different prognoses despite having the same diagnosis. Clustering has advantages over more traditional data analytics tools, such as logistic regression, and is better suited to tease out the complex relationships in a patient population that result from the interplay of biochemistry, genetics, environmental exposure to toxins, dietary habits, and numerous other variables. In other words, it's a tool that can facilitate a systems biology approach.

Christopher Seymour, with the University of Pittsburgh School of Medicine, and his colleagues used clustering to help decipher the relationship of several risk factors associated with sepsis.[6] Suspecting that the current definition of sepsis is probably too broad and of limited value in treating the disorder, they analyzed clinical data from over 20,000 patients—derived from electronic health records—who were diagnosed with sepsis using the Sepsis-3 criteria. Sepsis-3 takes into account body fluid cultures, antibiotic administration, and the presence of 2 or more Sequential Organ Failure Assessment (SOFA) points within the first 6 hours of presenting in the ED. With the assistance of the clustering technology, their goal was to look for patterns that suggested discrete phenotypes, for example, subgroups that may have distinct clinical and lab characteristics that might help establish more personalized treatment protocols and prognoses. The analysis included 29 clinical variables, including but not limited to C-reactive protein, erythrocyte sedimentation rate, respiratory rate, platelets, age, sodium, heart rate, white blood cell count, creatinine, comorbidities, bilirubin, hemoglobin, glucose, bicarbonate, oxygen saturation, blood urea nitrogen, troponin, temperature, albumin, lactate, and the international normalized ratio (INR).

Seymour et al.[6] found 4 unique phenotypes, each with different profiles based on these 29 variables, as well as different clinical outcomes. For instance, in-hospital mortality ranged from 2% to 32% among the 4 phenotypes. Similarly, there were differences in biomarkers among the groups. Finally, the investigators state: "These sepsis phenotypes can be identified at the time of patient presentation to the emergency department, and thus could be useful with regard to early treatment and enrollment in clinical trials." Of course, the key word in their conclusion is "could." Their analysis, although impressive, was nevertheless retrospective, suggesting that their findings are not quite ready for application at the bedside.

Clustering is also providing insights into the multidimensional nature of asthma and allergy. To appreciate the significance of this evidence, one first has to understand atopy, which is the tendency to develop immunologic reactions to common allergens. Currently, this propensity is determined by a person's prolonged immune response, as measured by immunoglobin E (IgE) antibody. Allergists typically arrive at a diagnosis of atopy by either measuring IgE levels in the blood or through skin prick tests to food and inhalant allergens. To date, a positive IgE antibody response is considered the strongest risk factor for predicting the eventual onset of asthma. However, since many individuals with elevated IgE levels never develop asthma, one has to question whether this marker needs to be reevaluated.

Applying ML methods to large patient populations reveals a much more nuanced understanding of atopy and how it influences one's susceptibility to asthma and related allergic conditions. These ML techniques, including clustering, suggest that there are several different phenotypes associated with atopy, with some more likely to predict the onset of clinical disease. Simpson et al., for instance, analyzed data from over 1,000 children who were part of a population birth cohort who had been recruited prenatally and followed prospectively in clinic until age 8 years.[7] During that time, the children were given numerous skin and blood tests to measure IgE levels, and the investigators used clustering to identify less obvious groupings of patients to detect unique phenotypes. The IgE tests and phenotypes were then compared to clinical findings, including symptoms, hospitalizations, lung function, and airway reactivity.

Simpson et al. discovered 5 distinct subgroups of patients with varying degrees of susceptibility to atopy[7]:

- Multiple Early vulnerability
- Multiple Late vulnerability
- Dust mite vulnerability
- Non–dust mite vulnerability
- No latent vulnerability

Children with Multiple Early vulnerability were strongly linked to clinical asthma when compared to the other 4 groups and compared to those labeled atopic based solely on the IgE testing. Similarly, lung function testing and airway reactivity was worse in the Multiple Early group. Without ML, all these patients would be lumped together into one homogenous group at risk for asthma, but with the help of ML, we can separate out subgroups that seem to follow different pathological pathways and clinical futures. Simpson et al. concluded: "It is not the presence or absence of specific IgE antibodies, but rather the pattern of the response (age at development, type and number of specific allergens involved) that has a fundamental effect on the clinical expression of asthma. It is of note that less than a third of children who would have been considered atopic at age 8 years using conventional diagnostic criteria were in the class most strongly associated with asthma (multiple early), whereas there was little appreciable increase in risk of asthma among those in the other classes."[7]

Of course, the existence of several asthma phenotypes does not in itself demonstrate that the disease has multiple causes, but a phenotype is the product of numerous genetic and environment factors and the work by Simpson et al. implies that it is more than a single disease, as reductionistic thinking would suggest.

Fontanella et al. found further evidence to show that relying on IgE levels is too simplistic.[8] Using the same population-based birth cohort used by Simpson et al.,[7] they discovered that allergic sensitization is not a single phenomenon, as suggested by elevated IgE response, but several different classes of sensitization. Fontanella et al. studied 461 children at age 11 years and measured specific IgE reactions to 112 allergen "components," that is, individual allergenic proteins. They found specific IgE reactions to 44 of these molecules in 46% of the children tested. They also found that the interactions among specific IgE reactions to several allergenic proteins also helped predict clinical asthma. For instance, among the 44 immune responses detected, 33 could be grouped into 7 clusters. Fontanella et al. concluded that "interactions among 18 pairs of allergen components predicted asthma with a good balance between sensitivity and specificity. For example, children with IgE antibodies to different allergenic proteins from both dog and cat, or horse and house dust mite, are at higher risk of developing asthma."[8]

Earlier in our discussion, we quoted Andrew Ahn's insight: "The temporal changes of a variable contain hidden, useful information about the overall system."[4] That observation is especially important in the context of asthma. Clinicians typically evaluate metrics such as peak expiratory flow (PER) in this patient population but too often rely on a single averaged weekly reading, which may hide underlying mechanisms and complex relationships. Measuring subtle changes in PER over time may help clinicians detect changes in the progression of the disease and prompt therapeutic adjustments. Thamrin et al. point out that "[c]linical recognition of temporal symptom patterns has already led to computerized peak flow algorithms for diagnosis of occupational asthma using machine learning."[9]

The Whole Is Greater than the Sum of Its Parts

While reductionism addresses biological systems by taking them apart, trying to detect their individual parts, one of the basic principles of network medicine states that the whole is greater than the sum of all of its parts. That realization encourages investigators to look for the effect of an entire forest of risk factors on health and disease rather than the individual trees. That concept also applies to the role of nutrition in health and disease. The professional and popular press is filled with headlines about the impact of sugar, salt, calories, and individual vitamins and minerals, but the human diet is composed of foods, not nutrients. One recent research project has examined the effect of entire food plans, in which it compared an ultra-processed diet to a whole foods regimen.[10,11]

This randomized controlled trial (RCT) enrolled 20 adults who were given diets with the same amounts of calories, macronutrients, sugar, sodium, and fiber and were allowed to consume as much or as little as they chose. They were confined to an NIH Clinical Center metabolic ward for 2 weeks, which allowed researchers to carefully measure their food consumption. Those on the refined food regimen took in about 500 kcal more a day, with increased intake of carbohydrates and fat. As expected, weight gain was closely correlated with calorie intake. Those on the processed diet gained about 1 kg, whereas subjects on the whole foods diet lost about 1 kg. Nutrition experts have argued for decades about the relative merits and dangers of individual nutrients, supported by a variety of observational studies, but this systems biology experiment is one of the first to establish a cause-and-effect relationship between the so-called junk food diet consumed by many persons in industrialized nations and the obesity epidemic we now face. Hall et al. theorize that the processed food diet may contribute to obesity by several mechanisms. They are "engineered to have supernormal appetive properties that may result in pathological eating behavior. Furthermore, ultra-processed foods are theorized to disrupt gut-brain signaling and may influence food reinforcement and overall intake via mechanisms distinct from the palatability or energy density of the food."[10] A typical menu for the ultra-processed regimen studied by Hall et al. consisted of Cheerios, milk, margarine, canned beef ravioli, white bread, cookies, diet lemonade, steak, instant potatoes, and canned corn. The unprocessed diet plan included plain yogurt, banana, apple, walnuts, homemade granola, spinach salad, grapes, beef roast, broccoli, pecans, salad, and sunflower seeds.[11]

Network Medicine's Essential Components

In systems biology, not only is the whole greater than the sum of its parts, the parts are much broader in scope than is typically the case in the reductionistic paradigm. In the past, researchers might study the role of single genes in the etiology of a disease, whereas a systems approach may analyze the entire genome and calculate polygenic risk scores. Similarly, old school thinking might focus on an individual intestinal microbe, whereas systems biology may study the entire microbiome. The essential components of this new school of thought also include metabolomics, proteomics, transcriptomics, exposome, and several other -omics. ML is playing a key role in understanding how these components influence health and disease.

A detailed metabolomics profile that takes advantage of ML tools may help pinpoint patients at risk for Type 2 diabetes before they develop full-blown disease. Gopal Peddinti, from the Institute for Molecular Bioscience, The University of Queensland in Australia, and his colleagues used multivariate logistic regression and regularized least squares (RLS) regression to develop a predictive model of diabetes. They chose the ML approach because conventional statistics tools such as univariate regression were inadequate to sift through and interpret all the interacting risk factors. The entire metabolomic profile consisted of 568 serum metabolites. They identified 9 metabolites that were negatively associated with progression to diabetes—in other words, they probably help protect patients from developing the disorder. They also detected 25 metabolites that were positively linked with progression to Type 2 diabetes.[12] Among the variables studied in this systems approach to predictive modeling were body mass index, waist circumference, fasting glucose and insulin, systolic and diastolic blood pressure, total cholesterol, HDL cholesterol, family history of Type 2 disease, physical activity level, and hypertension medication intake. Metabolites found to be positively associated with progression to diabetes included mannose, the amino acids histidine, isoleucine, valine, glutamate and glutamine, alpha-tocopherol (vitamin E), and glucose. Peddinti et al. also compared the metabolomics profile to a more traditional profile that only included clinical parameters such as sex, age, body mass index (BMI), fasting insulin, and family history. "The difference in the predictive performance between the metabolomics-only and the clinical-only models was statistically significant" ($P = 0.0009$).[12]

ML algorithms are making inroads in monitoring critical care patients at risk of cardiorespiratory instability as well. Currently, clinicians typically begin resuscitation efforts based on a drop in blood pressure, persistently elevated heart rate, and individual vital signs, including blood pressure, heart rate, oxygen saturation, and end-tidal CO_2. The problem with this approach is that it often does not detect cardiorespiratory insufficiency early on. Employing ML tools such as neural networks, support vector machines, and random forest modeling is moving critical care medicine into the future, allowing clinicians to predict who is most likely to deteriorate—in some cases, many hours sooner. Michael Pinsky, with the University of Pittsburgh Department of Critical Care

Medicine, and his associates have used neural network–based algorithms to develop a more precise way to predict the onset of cardiorespiratory instability using a ML system called Viscensia from OBS Medical. The software platform continually analyzes the combined patterns of 5 vital signs—BP, blood oxygen, temperature, respiratory rate, and HR, combining the data in unique ways to generate a single numerical value called the Safety index, also referred to as a vital signs index (VSI). Pinsky et al. demonstrated that a Safety index of above 3.2 was significantly correlated with instability that was independently established by clinical assessment. The earlier detection of emerging cardiorespiratory insufficiency also gave nurses time to intervene earlier.[13] "[T]he VSI alert occurred before clinically apparent instability in 80% of cases, with an advance time of 9.4 ± 9.2 min. Thus, such bedside-displayed VSI data can often detect the onset of cardiorespiratory insufficiency before overt symptoms are present and when coupled to appropriate immediate treatment plans markedly reduces patient instability."[13] The research from Pinsky et al. suggests that old-school severity scoring systems are woefully inadequate and fail to take into account the complex patient-specific interactions that transpire as each patient deteriorates. These interactions include a variety of autonomic, hormonal, and metabolic systems that demand a more wholistic approach to analysis.

The same scoring system inadequacies exist in oncology. One especially challenging area is assessing the likelihood of developing venous thromboembolism (VTE) in patients about to undergo chemotherapy. The Khorana score is currently being used to predict which patients are at greatest risk for VTE. It takes into account the type of cancer, the patient's platelet count before chemotherapy, hemoglobin levels, pre-chemotherapy leukocyte count, and BMI. Unfortunately, more than half of all cancer patients fall into the intermediate risk category using the Khorana score—not a very sensitive or specific metric upon which to base treatment decisions. Patrrizia Ferroni, at the San Raffaele Roma Open University, in Rome, Italy, and her associates have devised a ML-based assessment system that improves risk stratification.[14] Using kernel ML and random optimization (RO), they analyzed data from over 800 cancer patients to develop ML-RO predictors, which were then tested prospectively on 608 patients. Once again, the researchers took a broader approach to risk assessment, not limiting themselves to the variables included in the Khorana score. They included "age, sex, tumor site and stage, hematological attributes (including blood cell counts, hemoglobin, and neutrophil and platelet–lymphocyte ratios), fasting blood lipids, glycemic indexes, liver and kidney function, body mass index (BMI), Eastern Cooperative Oncology Group Performance Status (ECOG-PS), and supportive and anticancer drugs."[14] Their results, illustrated in Figure 6.4, demonstrated that ML-fueled risk analysis can outperform more traditional techniques.

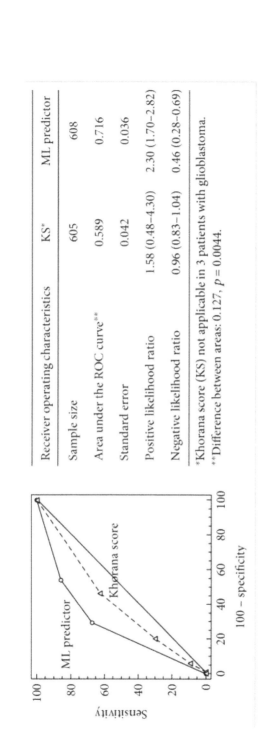

Receiver operating characteristics	KS*	ML predictor
Sample size	605	608
Area under the ROC curve**	0.589	0.716
Standard error	0.042	0.036
Positive likelihood ratio	1.58 (0.48–4.30)	2.30 (1.70–2.82)
Negative likelihood ratio	0.96 (0.83–1.04)	0.46 (0.28–0.69)

*Khorana score (KS) not applicable in 3 patients with glioblastoma.
**Difference between areas: 0.127, $p = 0.0044$.

Figure 6.4 Receiver operating characteristic curves generated from Khorana score (dashed line) and ML-RO VTE predictor (continuous line). (*Source:* Ferroni, P., Zanzotto, F. M., Scarpato, N., Riondino, S., Guadagni, F., and Roselli, M. [2017]. "Validation of a Machine Learning Approach for Venous Thromboembolism Risk Prediction in Oncology." *Disease Markers*, vol. 2017, ID 8781379.[14])

The research findings of Peddinti et al.,[12] Pinsky et al.,[13] and Ferroni et al.[14] are only the tip of the systems biology iceberg. They do take into account many of the other tools under consideration, including analysis of the genome, transcriptome, and microbiome.

Genome. Equally important are possible interactions among these components and their impact on human physiology. For example, among persons exposed to coffee, there is evidence to suggest that consumption of large quantities increases the risk of cardiovascular disease.[15,16] But a large-scale study that evaluated over 9 million individuals included in the UK Biobank cohort indicates a more nuanced interpretation of the research. It calculated hazard ratios (HR) for coffee intake and overall mortality to determine if caffeine metabolism, as influenced by single nucleotide polymorphisms (SNPs), including *AHR, CYP1A2, CYP2A6,* and *POR*, would affect the likelihood of death. On a 10-year follow-up, the analysis found that coffee consumption actually lowered the risk of death. Loftfield et al. concluded: "[T]he HRs for 6 or more cups per day ranged from 0.70 (95% CI, 0.53–0.94) to 0.92 (95%CI, 0.78–1.10), with no evidence of effect modification across strata of caffeine metabolism score."[17] In other words, the caffeine in coffee has no adverse effect on cardiovascular status for healthy individuals, regardless of whether they are slow or fast metabolizers, as indicated by their genetic makeup. From a systems biology perspective, the take home message is: A study of the interaction between the exposome and the genome eliminates caffeine as a likely contributor to cardiovascular disease, allowing investigators to look to some other ingredient in coffee as a possible culprit.

Studying network medicine's essential components is also providing useful insights into the nature of asthma, as we discussed earlier. Oligonucleotide microarrays and sequencing are homing in on single-nucleotide polymorphisms (SNPs) that may be involved in the pathophysiology of asthma, for instance. Some of the strongest evidence comes from genome-wide association studies (GWAS) that focus on the 17q21 locus, referring to chromosome 17—the lower q section, position 21. Four genes in this section of the chromosome— *ORMDL3, GSDMB, ZPBP2,* and *IKZF3*—have been linked to inflammatory response, a major problem for patients with asthma. GWAS also suggest that specific gene variants in the FLG gene contribute to atopic dermatitis in Europeans and Asians. The mutations are not usually found in Africans, as demonstrated by whole exome sequencing. (The exome is that fraction of the genome that contains protein-encoding DNA.)[18]

Transcriptome. Advances in transcriptomics are likewise providing insights into the pathophysiology of asthma. The transcriptome refers to RNA strands in our cells. Body proteins that carry out essential biological functions are created through a 3-step process: DNA provides the basic building blocks—the genes. These genes then go through the process of transcription, in which they are "converted" into RNA, which in turn undergoes the process of translation, which results in the generation of body proteins, including enzymes. As Bunyavanich and Shadt explain, "Transcriptomics offers a complementary and synergistic approach to GWAS for studying disease, as RNA reflects the more dynamic processes at play in a given tissue or tissues that underlie pathophysiology."[18] RNA sequencing has identified gene transcripts linked to eosinophilic esophagitis, a form of allergic inflammation of the esophagus, which are consistent with GWAS of patients with eosinophilic esophagitis. The GWAS also reveal relevant genetic variants on chromosome 5 (5q22). Similarly, RNA sequencing of airway biopsies has found several specific expressed genes, including *SLC26A4*, *POSTN*, and *BCL2*.

Microbiome. It is estimated that approximately 100 trillion microbes live on the human body. The way these visitors interact with the immune system influences our ability to fight off infections and resist allergic reactions. Among infants who have a less diverse mix of gut microbes, the likelihood of developing asthma by age 7 years is greater, as is atopic dermatitis during the first 18 months of life.[19–22] Giving expectant mothers probiotic supplements containing Bifidobacterium one month before they deliver and giving infants Bifidobacterium supplements for 6 months reduced the incidence of atopic dermatitis, when compared to controls.[23]

Systems Medicine Research

To home in on the many interacting causes of health and disease, researchers are now designing projects that take a much broader view of the population. One example of this systems approach is the All of Us Research Program sponsored by the U.S. National Institutes of Health. Previously called the Precision Medicine Initiative, it is collecting data on a long list of parameters that will give us a wholistic view of 1 million or more citizens. The metrics include demographics, medical visits, diagnoses, sociobehavioral information, procedures, medications, laboratory visits, vital signs, and physician notes. The investigation may include data about mental health, substance use, or HIV status, as well as results of urine, blood, and/or saliva tests. Unfortunately, it will be several years before results of that study are available. In the interim, there are smaller projects with the same wholistic agenda in mind.

The Institute for Systems Biology, for instance, conducted a study—the P100 Wellness Project—that enrolled over 100 individuals for 9 months and monitored their health with Fitbit devices, genome sequencing, clinical tests, and analysis of their metabolomes, proteomes, and microbiomes.[24] Their detailed analysis uncovered important patterns, relationships, and biomarkers that may be of value in tracking health and disease. Gamma-glutamyltyrosine, a metabolite of the enzyme gamma-glutamyl transferase, was interconnected with clinical analytes associated with cardiometabolic disease. Although the enzyme is a known marker for liver disease, diabetes, and cardiovascular risk, the metabolite is more predictive than the enzyme and may be useful as an independent marker, if these results can be confirmed by larger studies. Their data collection also allowed investigators to develop polygenic scores, based on GWAS, for 127 traits and diseases. Among the many findings, "genetic risk for inflammatory bowel disease was negatively correlated with plasma cystine."[24]

The P100 Wellness Project did not limit itself to collecting health data; it also provided participants with health coaching over the 9-month period. The goal was to recommend lifestyle changes that would alter biomarkers that have been linked to disease. The program reported 4 significant findings:

> *First, thousands of statistically significant inter-omic correlations were computed using personal, dense, dynamic data clouds to identify many associations that could be followed up with perturbation experiments. Second, we partitioned the correlations into data communities, which placed biomarkers in context within biological networks. . . . Third, we identified molecular correlates of polygenic disease risk scores computed from published GWAS data, revealing possible ways in which genetic predisposition is manifested through analyte changes. Finally, on average participants significantly improved their clinical biomarkers . . . during the course of this pilot study (e.g., type 2 diabetes and cardiovascular risk factors).*[24]

To truly reinvent CDS, we need to reinvent how we define disease and health. And systems biology is doing just that. As the evidence supporting systems biology grows stronger, we need to incorporate its insights into the latest CDS tools.

References

1. Ahn, A. C., Tewari, M., Poon, C. S., and Phillips, R. S. (2006). "The Limits of Reductionism in Medicine: Could Systems Biology Offer an Alternative?" *PLOS Medicine,* vol. 3, p. e201.
2. Loscalzo, J., Barabasi, A.-L., and Silverman, E. K. (2017). *Network Medicine: Complex Systems in Human Disease and Therapeutics*, 1st Edition. Cambridge (MA): Harvard University Press, p. 138.

3. Scarpa, J., Bruzelius, E., Doupe, P., Le, M., Faghmous, J., and Baum, A. (2019). "Assessment of Risk of Harm Associated with Intensive Blood Pressure Management Among Patients with Hypertension Who Smoke: A Secondary Analysis of the Systolic Blood Pressure Intervention Trial." *JAMA Open,* vol. 2, p. e190005.

4. Ahn, A. C., Tewari, M., Poon, C. S., and Phillips, R. S. (2006). "The Clinical Applications of a Systems Approach." *PLOS Medicine*, vol. 3, p. e209.

5. O'Rahilly, S., Turner, R. C., and Matthews, D. R. (1988). Impaired Pulsatile Secretion of Insulin in Relatives of Patients with Non-Insulin-Dependent Diabetes. *New England Journal of Medicine,* vol. 318, pp. 1225–1230.

6. Seymour, C. W., Kennedy, J. N., Wang, S., Chang, C. H., Elliott, C. F., Xu, Z., Berry, S., Clermont G., Cooper, G., Gomez, H., Huang, D. T., Kellum, J. A., Mi, Q., and Opal, S. M. (2019). "Derivation, Validation, and Potential Treatment Implications of Novel Clinical Phenotypes for Sepsis." *JAMA,* vol. 321, pp. 2003–2017.

7. Simpson, A., Tan, V. Y., Winn, J., Svensén, M., Bishop, C. M., Heckerman, D. E., Buchan,. I., and Custovic, A. (2010). "Beyond Atopy: Multiple Patterns of Sensitization in Relation to Asthma in a Birth Cohort Study." *Annals of Respiratory Critical Care Medicine,* vol. 181, pp. 1200–1206.

8. Fontanella, S., Frainay, C., Murray, C. S., Simpson, A., and Custovic, A. (2018). "Machine Learning to Identify Pairwise Interactions between Specific IgE Antibodies and Their Association with Asthma: A Cross-Sectional Analysis within a Population-Based Birth Cohort." *PLOS Medicine,* vol. 15, p. e1002691.

9. Thamrin, C., Frey, U., Kaminsky, D. A., Reddel, H. K., Seely, A. J., Suki, B., and Sterk, P. J. (2016). "Systems Biology and Clinical Practice in Respiratory Medicine. The Twain Shall Meet." *American Journal of Critical Care Medicine,* vol. 194, pp. 1053–1061.

10. Hall, K. D., Ayuketah, A., Brychta, R., Cai, H., Cassimatis, T., Chen, K. Y., Chung, S. T., Costa, E., and Courville, A. (2019). "Ultra-Processed Diets Cause Excess Calorie Intake and Weight Gain: An Inpatient Randomized Controlled Trial of Ad Libitum Food Intake." *Cell Metabolism,* vol. 30, pp. 67–77.

11. Liebman, B. (2019). "Are Ultra-Processed Foods Making Us Fat?" *Nutrition Action,* July/August, pp. 3–6.

12. Peddinti, G., Cobb, J., Yengo, L., Froguel, P., Kravić, J., Balkau, B., Tuomi, T., Aittokallio, T., and Groop, L. (2017). "Early Metabolic Markers Identify Potential Targets for the Prevention of Type 2 Diabetes." *Diabetologia,* vol. 60, pp. 1740–1750.

13. Pinsky, M. R., Clermont, G., and Hravnak, M. (2016). "Predicting Cardiorespiratory Instability." *Critical Care,* vol. 20, p. 70.

14. Ferroni, P., Zanzotto, F. M., Scarpato, N., Riondino, S., Guadagni, F., and Roselli, M. (2017). "Validation of a Machine Learning Approach for Venous Thromboembolism Risk Prediction in Oncology." *Disease Markers,* vol. 2017, ID 8781379.

15. Cornelis, M. C., El-Sohemy, A., Kabagambe, E. K., and Campos, H. (2016). "Coffee, CYP1A2 Genotype, and Risk of Myocardial Infarction." *JAMA,* vol. 295, pp. 1135–1141.

16. Palatini, P., Ceolotto, G., Ragazzo, F., Dorigatti, F., Saladini, F., Papparella, I., Mos, L., Zanata, G., and Santonastaso, M. (2009). "CYP1A2 Genotype Modifies the Association between Coffee Intake and the Risk of Hypertension." *Journal of Hypertension*, vol. 27, pp. 1594–1601.

17. Loftfield, E., Cornelis, M. C., Caporaso, N., Yu, K., Sinha, R., and Freedman, N. (2018). "Association of Coffee Drinking with Mortality by Genetic Variation in Caffeine Metabolism: Findings from the UK Biobank." *JAMA Internal Medicine*, vol. 178, pp. 1086–1097.

18. Bunyavanich, S. and Schadt, E. E. (2015). "Systems Biology of Asthma and Allergic Diseases: A Multiscale Approach." *Journal of Allergy and Clinical Immunology*, vol. 135, pp. 31–42.

19. Abrahamsson, T. R., Jakobsson, H. E., Andersson, A. F., Bjorksten, B., Engstrand, L., and Jenmalm, M. C. (2014). "Low Gut Microbiota Diversity in Early Infancy Precedes Asthma at School Age." *Clinical and Experimental Allergy*, vol. 44, pp. 842–850.

20. Abrahamsson, T. R., Jakobsson, H. E., Andersson, A. F., Bjorksten, B., Engstrand, L., and Jenmalm, M. C. (2012). "Low Diversity of the Gut Microbiota in Infants with Atopic Eczema." *Journal of Allergy and Clinical Immunology*, vol. 129, pp. 434–440. E1-2.

21. Wang, M., Karlsson, C., Olsson, C., Adlerberth, I., Wold, A. E., Strachan, D. P., Martricardi, P. M., Aberg, N., Perkin, M. R., Tripodi, S., Coates, A. R., Hesselmar, B., Saalman, R., Molin, G., and Ahrné, S. (2008). "Reduced Diversity in the Early Fecal Microbiota of Infants with Atopic Eczema." *Journal of Allergy and Clinical Immunology*," vol. 121, pp. 129–134.

22. Forno, E., Onderdonk, A. B., McCracken, J., Litonjua, A. A., Laskey, D., Delaney, M. L., Dubois, A. M., Gold, D. R., Ryan, L. M., Weiss, S. T., and Celedón, J. C. (2008). "Diversity of the Gut Microbiota and Eczema in Early Life." *Clinical and Molecular Allergy*, vol. 6, p. 11.

23. Enomoto, T., Sowa, M., Nishimori, K., Shimazu, S., Yoshida, A., Yamada, K., Nakagawa, T., Yanagisawa, N., Iwabuchi, N., Odamaki, T., Abe, F., Nakayama, J., and Xiao, J. Z. (2014). "Effects of Bifidobacterial Supplementation to Pregnant Women and Infants in the Prevention of Allergy Development in Infants and on Fecal Microbiota." *Allergology International*, vol. 63, pp. 575–585.

24. Price, N. D., Magis, A. T., Earls, J. C., Glusman, G., Levy, R., Lausted, C., McDonald, D. T., Kusebauch, U., Moss, C. L., Zhou, Y., Qin, S., Moritz, R. L., Brogaard, K., Omenn, G. S., Lovejoy, J. C., and Hood L. (2017). A Wellness Study of 108 Individuals Using Personal, Dense, Dynamic Data Clouds." *Nature Biotechnology*, vol. 35, pp. 747–756.

Chapter 7

Precision Medicine

Any discussion of the role of precision medicine in clinical decision making needs to start with a definition of terms. The US National Institutes of Health states: "There is a lot of overlap between the terms 'precision medicine' and 'personalized medicine.' According to the National Research Council, 'personalized medicine' is an older term with a meaning similar to 'precision medicine.' However, there was concern that the word 'personalized' could be misinterpreted to imply that treatments and preventions are being developed uniquely for each individual; in precision medicine, the focus is on identifying which approaches will be effective for which patients based on genetic, environmental, and lifestyle factors. The Council therefore preferred the term 'precision medicine' to 'personalized medicine.' However, some people still use the two terms interchangeably."[1] Some thought leaders, on the other hand, prefer the term personalized medicine, including the Penn State Institute of Personalized Medicine, the Charles Bronfman Institute for Personalized Medicine (located at the Icahn School of Medicine at Mount Sinai), and the Indiana Institute for Personalized Medicine at Indiana University School of Medicine. Another term that is often used in this context is P4 medicine, which refers to a form of healthcare that is at once predictive, preventative, personalized, and participatory. And the Mayo Clinic has weighed in on word choices with its Center for Individualized Medicine.

Still other thought leaders have a somewhat different perspective on personalized/precision medicine. That view states that most clinicians already use a personalized approach to patient care when they take into account a patient's age, gender, and family history to prescribe an antihypertensive drug,

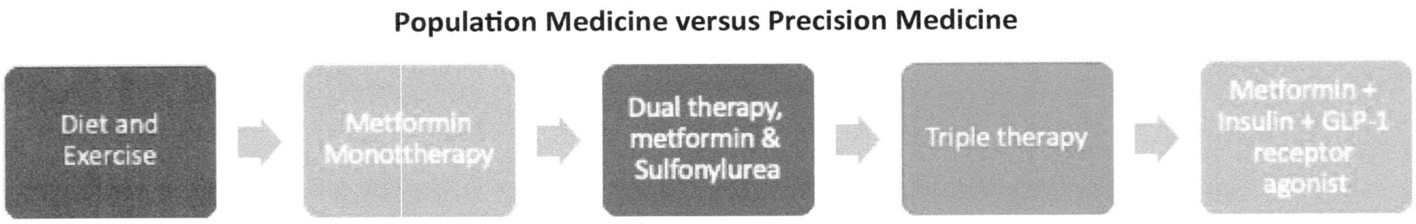

Population Medicine versus Precision Medicine

Figure 7.1   American Diabetes Association's Stepwise Approach to Type 2 Diabetes

for example. Although that approach may be personalized to a degree, it ignores numerous risk factors that may influence an individual's response to medication. In this view, a precision medicine approach would take into account the patient's genome, using any pathologic mutations to further tailor their regimen. Similarly, a more precise treatment regimen might take into account the individual's dietary habits and their exposure to environmental toxins and occupational hazards, to name only a few variables.

This distinction is apparent when one looks at the American Diabetes Association's treatment algorithm for type 2 diabetes.[2] Its initial recommendation calls for diet and exercise to control blood glucose levels. If that fails, the next step is metformin monotherapy, followed by more aggressive medication regimens, as illustrated in Figure 7.1. Although this 5-step approach may not be one-size-fits-all medicine, it does not take into account numerous other risk factors and variables that should inform the treatment of each patient. Psychosocial stress is known to influence a person's metabolic control and yet the ADA algorithm does not take it into account. Neither does it factor in any nutritional variables such as magnesium deficiency, a patient's financial status, and their ability to afford medication and nutritious food, or even such basics as their ability to travel back and forth to the doctor's office. Factoring in these variables would make a diabetes algorithm much more precise.

The ADA algorithm may improve somewhat on one-size-fits-all medicine, but at best, it still touches on only a fraction of the variables that impact a diabetic patient's life. Equally important, it ignores root causes. As we discussed in Chapter 6, diabetes is much more than abnormal glucose metabolism, which suggests that administering a drug that simply lowers blood glucose levels is only part of the solution. The same dilemma occurs in many other degenerative diseases.

Rheumatoid arthritis (RA) is a prime example. The etiology of RA remains a mystery, although we do know that the pathological process results in secretion of many immune factors, including tumor necrosis factor-α (TNF-α). But TNF-α is only an intermediate cause of the disease. Nevertheless, the most widely used class of drugs used to treat RA inhibits the body's production of this immune factor. Although these medications have proven very effective in relieving signs and symptoms, they do not target the root cause of the disease, and they also disrupt the body's normal immune response to inflammation. As Bruce Kirkham, MD, explains in *UpToDate*: "TNF-alpha is an important component of the immune system's response to a variety of infections, and use of TNF-alpha inhibitors has been associated with an increased risk of serious infections. These include bacterial infections (particularly pneumonia), zoster, tuberculosis, and opportunistic infections."[3] Contrast this therapeutic approach to that used to resolve diet-induced iron deficiency anemia. Iron supplements and an iron-rich diet are prescribed to address its root cause. The difference between these two approaches is illustrated in Figures 7.2A and 7.2B.[4] Put another way, the treatment of dietary iron deficiency anemia is a form of precise medicine. The treatment of RA with TNF-α inhibitors is not.

As we mentioned in Chapter 6, the All of Us Research Program sponsored by the US National Institutes of Health, previously called the Precision Medicine Initiative, is collecting data on a long list of parameters that will give us a holistic view of 1 million or more citizens. The metrics include demographics, genetic predisposition, medical visits, diagnoses, sociobehavioral information, procedures, medications, laboratory visits, vital signs, and physician notes. This project will address many of the shortcomings of population-based medicine.

Addressing Genetic Predisposition

Since heredity plays such a central role in susceptibility to disease, it's no surprise to learn that most precision medicine projects include a genomics component. These initiatives face numerous challenges:

- The genomic data needs to be accurately imported into an electronic health record (EHR) or some other digital conduit that clinicians can quickly access.
- The data that clinicians receive needs to be actionable, that is, it has to have practical implications that inform diagnosis and treatment for each patient.
- Doctors and nurses have to be capable of correctly interpreting the genomic findings, which requires a deeper understanding of genetic medicine than many clinicians currently possess.
- The genomic services need to be covered by third-party payors.

An in-depth discussion of the technological issues involved in importing genomic data into EHRs is beyond the scope of this book; however, several investigators are studying whether primary care physicians can manage this data once it's available. In one pilot study, physicians were given access to one group of patients' family history along with whole genome-sequencing reports that had previously been reviewed by genetic experts; a second group only provided a family history report to their physician.[5] The genetic reports included monogenic disease risk (MDR) results, risk estimates for cardiometabolic traits, and pharmacogenomic associations. Eleven of the patients whose family history and genomic data were available had a risk of developing a monogenic disorder (22% of the 50 healthy patients in the first group), two of which had evidence of clinical disease. Geneticists rated the physicians' management of monogenic

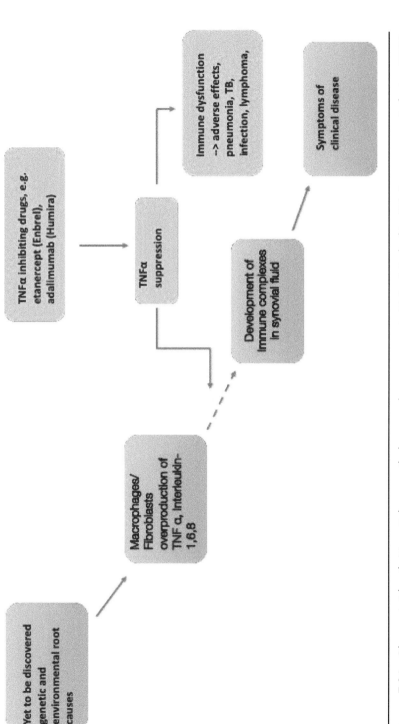

Figure 7.2A Rheumatoid arthritis: etiology, pathology, and management. *Note:* interleukin (IL); tumor necrosis factor (TNF). *(Source: Adapted from Cerrato, P. and Halamka, J. [2018]. Realizing the Promise of Precision Medicine: The Role of Patient Data, Mobile Technology, and Consumer Engagement. Elsevier/Academic Press. Used with permission.[4]*

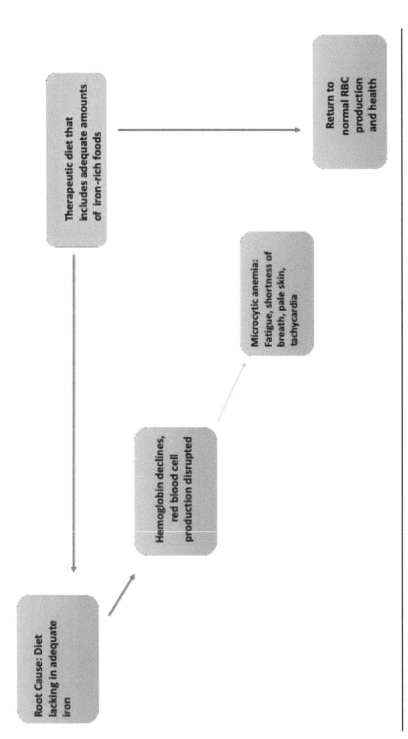

Figure 7.2B Iron deficiency anemia: etiology, pathology, and cure. (*Source:* Adapted from Cerrato, P. and Halamka, J. [2018]. *Realizing the Promise of Precision Medicine: The Role of Patient Data, Mobile Technology, and Consumer Engagement.* Elsevier/Academic Press. Used with permission.[4])

disease risk information as appropriate in 8 patients (73%) and inappropriate in 2 cases (18%).

Although these findings suggest that primary care physicians (PCPs) may be capable of handling the results of genomic sequencing, two important caveats must be kept in mind when interpreting the study. The clinicians were essentially "spoon fed" the results of the gene sequencing. Vassy et al. explain: "Raw data files were analyzed in the Partners Laboratory for Molecular Medicine, where molecular geneticists classified variants selected for possible clinical relevance from a curated list of 4,631 disease-associated genes into five categories: benign, likely benign, uncertain significance . . . , likely pathogenic (LP), and pathogenic (P)."[5] In addition, the nine PCPs who participated in the experiment received 4 hours of case-based online training and 2 one-hour in-person group classes to help them understand genomics and the reports they were to receive.

Studies such as this underscore the need for better physician education. Fortunately, there is reason for optimism as we see a growing number of educational programs springing up in the United States. Genomic training is gradually finding its way into medical school curriculums. Stanford University was the first to integrate the topic into its programs in 2011. Several medical schools have followed its example. In 2013, the Inter-Society Coordinating Committee for Physician Education in Genomics (ISCC) was also launched to improve physician education in this area. Its goal is to instill 5 key skills in recent medical school graduates[6]:

- Obtaining a family history
- Ordering the right genomic tests
- Prescribing the appropriate therapy based on test results
- Understanding somatic genetics
- Understanding microbial genomics

In addition to medical school training programs, there are several continuing medical education initiatives that now focus on genomics, including in-person training sessions at the Icahn School of Medicine at Mount Sinai and the Electronic Medical Records and Genomics Network.

Pharmacogenomics: Precision Medicine's Low-Hanging Fruit

Of all the genomics data now emerging, pharmacogenomic data is probably the most immediately useful for clinicians seeking to provide more precise and personalized patient care. Although decision makers and regulators that control the purse strings in healthcare continue to debate the cost effectiveness of ordering pharmacogenomic testing, several future-minded clinicians and technologists are already building the infrastructure that will make it a reality at the community level. The goal of that infrastructure is to give clinicians quick access to a patient's gene/drug interactions in the EHR or through an EHR plug-in that will allow them to adjust medication dosage as needed.

One such project, spearheaded by R. H. Dolin and associates at Elimu Informatics, produced a prototype for a pharmacogenomics clinical decision support (PGx CDS) service and linked it to an existing commercially available EHR system. The PGx CDS system relies on Fast Healthcare Interoperability Resources (FHIR) and CDS Hooks.[7] The system is triggered when a clinician places a medication order in the EHR. Once that occurs, the system searches for relevant genetic data in a Genomic Archiving and Communication System (GACS) and then notifies the prescribing clinician about any relevant recommendations. If there are no pharmacogenomic test results in the patient's records, the PGx CDS system recommends that a test be ordered when indicated.

Unfortunately, regulators and third-party payors continue to debate the term "when indicated." And since it is very unlikely that clinicians will be reimbursed for the vast majority of PGx tests as we go to press, very few of them order them. But it is getting more difficult for decision makers to ignore the mounting evidence that justifies the use of pharmacogenomic testing. Dolin et al. sum up this evidence:

> PGx use cases are of particular interest because over half of all primary care patients are exposed to PGx relevant drugs. Studies have found that 7% of U.S. Food and Drug Administration (FDA)-approved medications and 18% of the 4 billion prescriptions written in the United States per year are affected by actionable PGx variants; that nearly all individuals (98%) have at least one known, actionable variant by current Clinical Pharmacogenetics Implementation Consortium (CPIC) guidelines; and that when 12 pharmacogenes with at least one known, actionable, inherited variant are considered, over 97% of the U.S. population has at least one high-risk diplotype with an estimated impact on nearly 75 million prescriptions.[7]

Mayo Clinic is at the forefront in the effort to bring PGx testing into mainstream medicine. It has partnered with the Baylor College of Medicine to sequence 77 pharmacogenes from 10,000 patients who are being cared for at the Clinic in Rochester, Minnesota. Some of the results of these tests have been inserted into the clinic's EHR so that clinicians can act on them. The EHR already has 19 drug/gene pairs targeted, providing clinicians with decision-support alerts as needed.[8] Richard Weinshilboum, MD, professor of pharmacology and medicine at the Mayo Clinic, believes that within 5–10 years, PGx testing will become standard of care and give clinicians an important tool to let them personalize dosages for each patient. "It sounds like a fairy tale, but it will come," Weinshilboum says. "Eventually, the insurance companies will realize that they're going to ultimately save money over time by virtue of optimizing the drug therapy of the patient."[9]

Similar to many leading healthcare organizations, Mayo Clinic has discovered that folding PGx testing data into patients' records is no easy task. There are many clinical, procedural, and technical challenges to deal with. The Clinic has addressed these issues with an innovative system it calls Genomic Indicators (Gen-Ind).[10] It charts PGx phenotypes in the Gen-Ind repository instead of inserting the data in the EHR's problem or allergy list. Typically, the genomic test results come from the Clinic's Personalized Genomics Laboratory and are linked to the EHR (Epic) as PDFs and structured data in the form of genotype/phenotype. Pedro Caraballo and his colleagues describe additional features of the new system: "Additional functionality includes easy access; clinician ability to add comments and security to control who can add, edit, delete, or view them; automatic documentation from PGx laboratory results; manual documentation; hyperlinks to access the original PGx lab report (PDF); and multiple links to additional educational information."[10] The bottom line for clinicians: The new digital tool displays PGx phenotype and actionable information about potential risks.

This type of program seems like a lifetime away for most physicians and patients who would benefit from PGx testing now. The US Food and Drug Administration publishes a list of more than 160 drugs that contain pharmacogenomic information in their package inserts. In the preface to the drug list, it states: "Pharmacogenomics can play an important role in identifying responders and non-responders to medications, avoiding adverse events, and optimizing drug dose. Drug labeling may contain information on genomic biomarkers and can describe:

- Drug exposure and clinical response variability
- Risk for adverse events
- Genotype-specific dosing

The labeling for some, but not all, of the products includes specific actions to be taken based on the biomarker information."[11]

Despite the FDA's recognition that these drug/gene interactions can have clinical implications, its position is at odds with the policies of the Centers for Medicare and Medicaid Services, which determines which of these tests it will pay for. Federal regulations require CMS to only pay for laboratory procedures that it deems "reasonable and necessary" and that does not include most of gene/drug interactions that have been confirmed by scientists.

The cytochrome P-450 family of liver enzymes is responsible for metabolizing many drugs, and mutations to the genes that control the synthesis of these enzymes can have a significant impact on how an individual responds to drugs that are broken down by these enzymes. Such genetic variants can result in a patient becoming a slow metabolizer, in which case the drug will have a prolonged therapeutic effect, risking toxicity, or a fast metabolizer, in which case a patient may experience a sub-therapeutic effect from said drug.

Within this series of hepatic enzymes, Medicare coverage is only provided for CYP2D6 testing for patients who are starting treatment on the antidepressants amitriptyline or nortriptyline, and for anyone taking tetrabenazine in doses above 50 mg/day. The agency will also cover CYP2C19 testing for patients starting or restarting clopidogrel, but only if they have acute coronary syndrome and are undergoing percutaneous coronary intervention (PCI).[12]

Although private health insurers typically follow Medicare guidelines, at least one major payor has broken ranks and is now moving into the future of drug sensitivity testing. In August, 2019, UnitedHealthcare announced that it would pay for PGx testing for patients with major depression and anxiety disorder who have failed to respond at least once to drug therapy. The new policy is consistent with research that has found that about 50% of patients do not see benefits from the first antidepressant they are prescribed.[13] UnitedHealthcare's medical policy states: "The use of pharmacogenetic Multi-Gene Panels to guide therapy decisions is proven and medically necessary for antidepressants and antipsychotics medication when ALL of the following criteria are met:

- The individual has a diagnosis of major depressive disorder or anxiety; and
- The individual has failed at least one prior medication to treat their condition; and
- The Multi-Gene Panel has no more than 15 relevant genes."[14]

PGx testing is not only valuable in determining which patients are most likely to react poorly to specific drugs. It has also been shown to help pinpoint individuals who will respond best to cancer therapy. Testing for the genes for epidermal growth factor receptor (EGFR), for instance, will help determine how the drug erlotinib is used in patients with advanced non-small cell lung cancer; similarly, KRAS testing is valuable in patients being considered for cetuximab for advanced colorectal cancer. Christine Y. Lu, with the Precision Medicine Translational Research Center at Harvard Medical School, and her colleagues reviewed reimbursement policies for pharmacogenomic testing for cancer patients and found that it is common for Medicare contractors and private insurers to pay for KRAS, EGFR, and BRAF tests.[15]

The Future of Precision/Personalized Medicine

Genomics may be an important component of precision medicine, but it is only one of many essentials. In the case of Type 2 diabetes, for instance, there is currently no genetic profile that will pinpoint the disease or effectively manage it. Nonetheless, a personalized approach can go a long way toward improving patient outcomes. To home in on patients' needs, clinicians need to be aware of emerging problems, including complications that occur while they are hospitalized. Traditionally, this is accompanied with a specialty consult, which is a slow, inefficient process. At the University of California at San Francisco (UCSF) Diabetes, they have developed a more streamlined approach, called a targeted automatic e-consultation (TACo), to meet the needs of individual patients who require special attention.[16] At UCSF, the EHR system automatically screens all inpatients and tags patients who meet 1 of 4 criteria for one of these e-consults:

- Type 1 diabetes
- The presence of an insulin pump
- 2 or more blood glucose readings at or above 225 mg/dl
- Blood glucose level below 70 mg/dl in the past 24 hours

The EHR system displays these readings in a dashboard that shows glucose trends, the doses of insulin and oral hypoglycemic drugs the patient is taking, and any medications he or she is using that can influence glucose levels. The dashboard also displays fluid and nutritional information and lab test results that the diabetologist may find useful. Consultants then write up a brief note with their recommendations. The entire process takes 2–5 minutes. Wachter et al. state that an evaluation of over 1,000 TACos found a 39% drop in the percentage of patients with hyperglycemia and a 36% decline in hypoglycemic events when compared to patients who were not processed through this new approach.[16]

Of course, the future of precision medicine goes beyond automatic e-consults. It must even go beyond the long list of variables and risk factors currently being measured by the in All of Us project. Obesity, diabetes, and heart disease, three of the most destructive diseases in the developed world, cannot be addressed with good science and data analytics alone. They require clinicians and patients come to terms with numerous social and behavioral roadblocks. Stacey Chang, MD, from the Design Institute of Health, Dell Medical School, and Thomas Lee, MD, Harvard Medical School, sum up the much-needed prescription: These problems are "better addressed through a series of meaningful interactions focused on motivation, engagement, empowerment, conviction, and resilience. These interactions occur in the home, at work, at play in the communities (and sometimes in clinics) . . ."[17] At the grass roots level, that means screening all Medicaid patients to assess their social needs, for instance, an initiative that occurs at Brigham and Women's Hospital, and then acting on those assessments to bring in community health workers and others to address them. Similarly, there is a communication skills training program at the Cleveland Clinic, Texas Children's Hospital, and a few other forward-thinking institutions to reorient physicians to this better way of interacting with patients.

Precision medicine 2.0 also needs to take into account patient preferences when calculating the measurements it uses to rate the success of its interventions. Currently, we use metrics such as hemoglobin A1c, body mass index, and hospital readmission rates, which certainly have a role in determining patient outcomes. But if we were to ask Ms. Jones what is really important, it's likely she would use very different metrics: "Will I be able to dance at my daughter's wedding?" is probably more important. A truly personalized patient/doctor exchange needs to explore these kinds of real-world issues as well.

The future of precise/personalized patient care will take advantage of N of 1 clinical trials, that is, studies of single patients, as well. As we have explained in previous publications, large-scale randomized controlled trials (RCTs) have their limitations and can easily miss outliers who respond to a treatment protocol that does not generate statistically significant results for the average patient. One way to address this shortcoming is to perform a double-blind randomized trial on an individual patient. Aggregating the results of several N of 1 trials is an even more creative way to detect therapeutic effects that only affect a small number of individuals. To demonstrate the feasibility of such a methodology, Bas C. Stunnenberg, MD, and his colleagues at Radboud University Medical Center, Nijmegen, the Netherlands,[18] studied the effects of mexiletine on muscle stiffness of patients with a rare neurological disease called nondystrophic myotonia (NDM). NDM affects fewer than 1 in 100,000 persons and is caused by a genetic defect that disrupts normal skeletal muscle sodium and chloride channels. Their trial demonstrated that the drug was effective in relieving symptoms, when compared to placebo.

There is almost no limit to the potential role of precision medicine in reinventing clinical decision support. That includes its role in information retrieval. One of the problems that clinicians face when trying to locate the most relevant research for patient care is the massive amount of literature they must comb through. Finding that proverbial needle in a haystack for individual patients with difficult-to-treat conditions can consume more time than the average physician or nurse has. Saeid Balaneshinkordan and Alexander Kotov, with the Department of Computer Science at Wayne State University in Detroit, have developed a Bayesian approach to information retrieval to help improve medical literature queries. Their goal is to help clinicians find personalized treatment options for complex diseases, using their genomic data.[19]

The researchers used query expansion in situations in which clinicians input 2 types of information into a query. (Query expansion is a process in information retrieval that consists of selecting and adding terms to the user's query with the goal of minimizing query-document mismatch and thereby improving retrieval performance.) They provide a short write-up of the patient's case, including the type of cancer, demographics, and signs and symptoms. Then they input any mutations they have discovered into the system. The new retrieval system ranks the literature search results using a probabilistic approach that maps the genetic variants in each query to biomedical concepts related to the entire query, with the help of query expansion.

The value of query expansion can be better appreciated when one considers some of the challenges of conducting a targeted literature search. The two main challenges are the length of the patient description, which often takes up pages of medical history, symptoms, test results, and diagnoses. The second roadblock is the vocabulary mismatch that often occurs when clinicians rely on computers to interpret their words—an elevated body temperature can be called fever, pyrexia, or abnormal temperature, for example. Among the extraction tools that can be used to solve the problem are MetaMap, DNorm, and query expansion. As Balaneshinkordan and Kotov explain: "Query expansion, which aims at finding terms or phrases that are semantically related to a given query and can be added to it to retrieve more or improve the ranking of relevant documents, is one of the most effective approaches for improving the quality of results in IR systems for CDS."[19] Testing the new model on a subset of MEDLINE article and abstracts for the American Association for Cancer Research and the American Society of Clinical Oncology proceedings, the investigators were able to generate more accurate and focused query results.

Regardless of the words we use to describe precision/personalized/individualized medicine, all the evidence points us to a future that will reinvent clinical decision support and transform patient care in ways that are hard to imagine even today.

References

1. Genetics Home Reference. (2019, September 10). "What Is Precision Medicine?" Retrieved from https://ghr.nlm.nih.gov/primer/precisionmedicine/definition
2. Inzucchi, S. E., Bergenstal, R. M., Buse, J. B., Diamant, M., Ferrannini, E., Nauck, M., Peters, A. L., Tsapas, A., Wender, R., and Matthews, D. R. (2015). "Management of Hyperglycemia in Type 2 diabetes, 2015: A Patient-Centered Approach: Update to a Position Statement of the American Diabetes Association and the European Association for the Study of Diabetes." *Diabetes Care,* vol 38, no. 1, pp. 140–149.

3. Kirkham, B. (2016, April 26)."Tumor Necrosis Factor-Alpha Inhibitors: An Overview of Adverse Effects. UpToDate." Retrieved from https://www.uptodate.com/contents/tumor-necrosis-factor-alpha-inhibitors-an-overview-of-adverse-effects.

4. Cerrato, P. and Halamka, J. (2018). *Realizing the Promise of Precision Medicine: The Role of Patient Data, Mobile Technology, and Consumer Engagement.* Elsevier/Academic Press.

5. Vassy, J. L., Christensen, K. D., Schonman, E. F., Blout, C. L., Robinson, J. O., Krier, J. B., and Diamond, P. M. (2017). "The Impact of Whole-Genome Sequencing on the Primary Care and Outcomes of Healthy Adult Patients: A Pilot Randomized Trial." *Annals of Internal Medicine,* vol. 167, pp. 159–169.

6. Rubanovich, C. K., Cheung, C., Mandel, J., and Bloss, C. S. (2018). "Physician Preparedness for Big Genomic Data: A Review of Genomic Medicine Education Initiatives in the United States." *Human Molecular Genetics,* vol. 27, pp. R250–258.

7. Dolin, R. H., Boxwala, A., and Shalaby, J. (2018). "A Pharmacogenomics Clinical Decision Support Service Based on FHIR and CDS Hooks." *Methods of Information in Medicine,* vol. 57, pp. e115–e123.

8. Bielinski, S. (n.d.). "Pharmacogenomics: Right 10K study. Mayo Clinic Center for Individualized Medicine." Retrieved from https://www.mayo.edu/research/centers-programs/center-individualized-medicine/patient-care/clinical-studies/pharmacogenomics-right-10k. Accessed October 10, 2019.

9. Shute, D. (n.d.). "Pharmacogenomics to Eventually Touch Every Patient, Everywhere, Expert Says. Precision Medicine Institute." Accessed October 10, 2019, from https://precision-medicine-institute.com/pharmacogenomics-to-eventually-touch-every-patient-everywhere-expert-says

10. Caraballo, P. J., Sutton, J. A., Giri, J., Wright, J. A., Nicholson, W. T., Kullo, I. J., Parkulo, M. A., Bielinski, S. J., and Moyer, A. M. (2019). "Integrating Pharmacogenomics into the Electronic Health Record by Implementing Genomic Indicators." *Journal of Medical Informatics Association,* Oct 7. pii: ocz177. [epub ahead of print.] Retrieved from https://www.ncbi.nlm.nih.gov/pubmed/?term=Integrating+pharmacogenomics+into+the+electronic+health+record+by+implementing+genomic+indicators

11. FDA. (2019, September 3). FDA Table of Pharmacogenomic Biomakers in Drug Labeling. Retrieved from https://www.fda.gov/drugs/science-and-research-drugs/table-pharmacogenomic-biomarkers-drug-labeling

12. Frequently Asked Questions. Genelex. Accessed October 11, 2019, from https://www.genelex.com/faqs/?_ga=2.56623912.300664125.1570708476-1193212891.1570708476#insurance

13. Trivedi, M. H., Rush, A. J., Wisniewski, S. R., Nierenberg, A. A., Warden, D., Ritz, L., Norquist, G., Howland, R. H., Lebowitz, B., McGrath, P. J., Shores-Wilson, K., Biggs, M. M., Balasubramani, G. K., Fava, M., and STAR*D Study Team. (2006). "Evaluation of Outcomes with Citalopram for Depression Using Measurement-Based Care in STAR*D: Implications for Clinical Practice." *American Journal of Psychiatry,* vol. 163, pp. 28–40.

14. "Pharmacogenetic Testing." (2019, October 1). UnitedHealthcare Commercial

Medical Policy. Retrieved from   https://www.uhcprovider.com/content/dam/provider/docs/public/policies/comm-medical-drug/pharmacogenetic-testing.pdf

15. Lu, C. Y., Loomer, S., Ceccarelli, R., Mazor, K. M., Sabin, J., Clayton, E. W., Ginsburg, G. S., and Wu, A. C. (2018). "Insurance Coverage Policies for Pharmacogenomic and Multi-Gene Testing for Cancer." *Journal for Personalized Medicine,* vol. 16, p. E19.

16. Wachter, R. M., Judson, T. J., and Mourad, M. (2019). "Reimagining Specialty Consultation in the Digital Age: The Potential Role of Targeted Automatic Electronic Consultations." *JAMA,* vol. 322, pp. 399–340.

17. Chang, S. and Lee, T. H. (2018). " Beyond Evidence-Based Medicine." *New England Journal of Medicine,* vol. 379, pp. 1983–1985.

18. Stunnenberg, B. C., Raaphorst, J., Groenewoud, H. M., Statland, J. M., Griggs, R. C., Woertman, W., Stegeman, D. F., Timmermans, J., and Trivedi, J. (2018). "Effect of Mexiletine on Muscle Stiffness in Patients with Nondystrophic Myotonia Evaluated Using Aggregated N-of-1 Trials." *JAMA,* vol. 320, pp. 2344–2353.

19. Balaneshinkordan, S. and Kotov, A. (2019). " Bayesian Approach to Incorporating Different Types of Biomedical Knowledge Bases into Information Retrieval Systems for Clinical Decision Support in Precision Medicine." *Journal of Biomedical Informatics,* vol. 98, p. 103238.

Chapter 8

Reinventing Clinical Decision Support: Case Studies

Many of the emerging digital tools we discussed in this book are poised to transform healthcare in profound ways, improving the diagnosis of eye disease, helping to detect skin cancer, and offering more personalized ways to manage severe sepsis and many other disorders. But these breakthrough technologies sometimes overshadow other artificial intelligence (AI)–fueled innovations that address some of the more mundane—but essential—aspects of patient care. Although these initiatives may not make front page headlines, they nonetheless play an important role in the lives of clinicians and patients.

Beth Israel Deaconess Medical Center (BIDMC), a Harvard Medical School–affiliated teaching hospital, is among the many innovators that are taking a leading role in this arena, using machine learning (ML) and other forms of AI to improve day-to-day operations. For example, BIDMC is using ML to improve the scheduling of its 41 operating rooms and to synchronize the schedules of the ORs to facilitate operational flow within the rooms themselves. As Figure 8.1 illustrates, the hospital is able to scan pre-surgical documents, including History and Physical (H&P) forms, so that they are available to the OR staff. Although scanning patient consent forms and other documents may not seem as "sexy" as using a retinal camera and ML-based algorithms to screen for diabetic retinopathy, having to delay a surgical procedure because of a missing document can be expensive and wastes valuable resources. Figure 8.2 provides

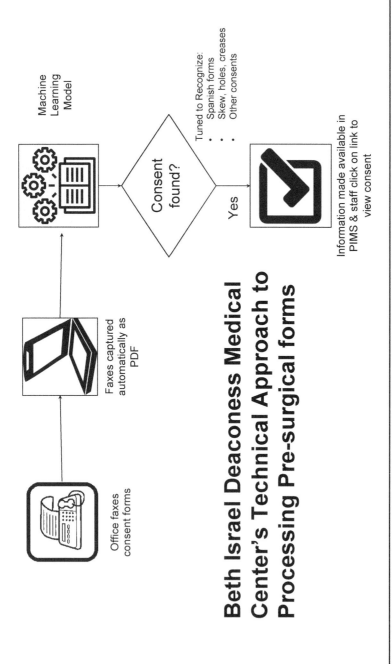

Figure 8.1 Beth Israel Deaconess Medical Center uses machine learning (ML) to convert office faxes containing patient consent forms into computer readable data, which is then imported into the patient's chart and made available to doctors, nurses, pharmacists, social workers, case managers. PIMS = Perioperative Information Management System. (Courtesy of Beth Israel Deaconess Medical Center.)

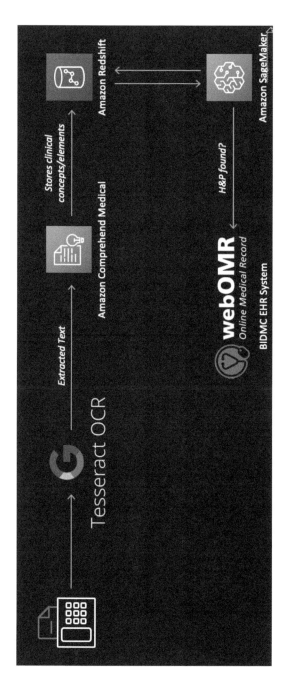

Figure 8.2 The process of moving consent form text into a patient's electronic health record (EHR) typically begins with an incoming fax, which then must be "translated" with the help of an optical character recognition program (Tesseract OCR). OCR software converts printed characters into digital text. The extracted text is sent to Amazon Comprehend Medical, which extracts relevant clinical concepts and elements and sends them to a cloud-based data warehouse called Amazon Redshift. Redshift in turn shares content with SageMaker, which builds and deploys machine learning (ML) models. With the help of these models, patient consent forms and H&P forms can be imported into webOMR. WebOMR is the inpatient EHR system used by Beth Israel Deaconess and other Harvard affiliated hospitals. (Courtesy of Beth Israel Deaconess Medical Center.)

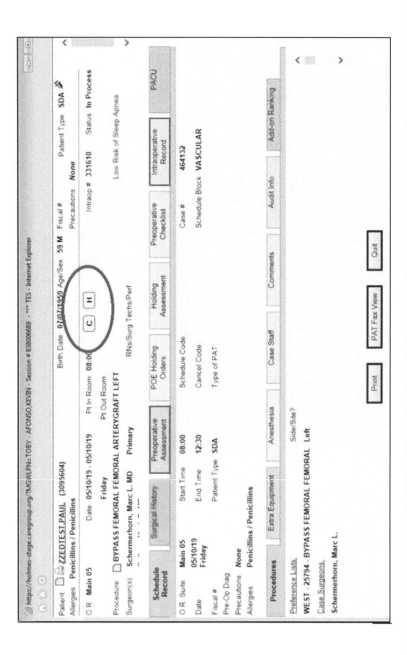

Figure 8.3 A sample patient chart that includes verification that their consent form and H&P form have been entered into the system. (Courtesy of Beth Israel Deaconess Medical Center.)

more details on the technology being used by the medical center to achieve this aim. As the Figure 8.2 caption explains, BIDMC uses Amazon Comprehend Medical to facilitate the scheduling procedure. The service extracts medical terms and insights used by the ML system to identify H&P forms. (More details on Amazon Comprehend Medical are discussed in the inset text below.)

Understanding Amazon Comprehend Medical

One of the major obstacles to using patient information to make clinical decisions is the fact that so much of it is "trapped" in unstructured form. To clinicians unfamiliar with how computers interpret patient data, this will no doubt sound like technobabble, but the simple truth is that computers have a hard time interpreting data that is not neatly packaged in an electronic health record (EHR) system's drop-down menus and other structured entry points. Doctors' narrative notes, summaries of clinical research, and other "messy" text pose a problem that, until recently, could not be solved. Natural language processing (NLP), which is familiar to any physician who uses a speech recognition program to record their dictation, serves as the basis for Amazon Comprehend Medical (ACM) as well. Details on ACM are available on their web site at https://aws.amazon.com/comprehend/medical/[1]

Of course, most hospital administrators have little interest in how the technology works. Their primary concern is: Will it actually improve efficiency and save man-hours. Figure 8.3 illustrates how the ML-based system is used in an individual patient's chart. Giving clinicians access to this automated platform has generated tangible benefits. Since March 1, 2018, over 10,000 patient consent forms have been identified with the system, saving hundreds of hours. Similarly, since May 21, 2019, over 50 H&P forms have been identified, saving many hours of manual work.

Improving Patient Scheduling, Optimizing ED Functioning

Another area of concern for both administrators and clinicians is patient no-shows. BIDMC has once again taken the lead, developing a ML system to help predict who is most likely to keep their office appointments and who is not. The platform takes advantage of Apache MXNet's application programming interface (API) and Amazon's SageMaker, which help providers build, train,

(A)

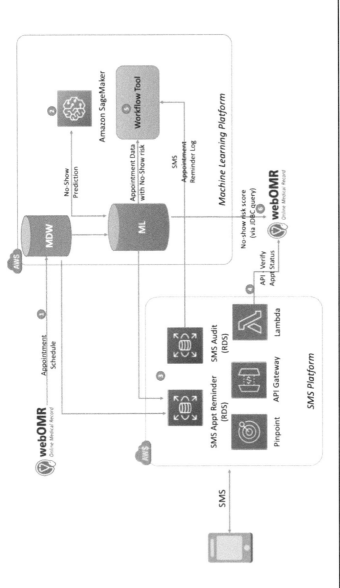

Figure 8.4 (A & B) To help predict the ambulatory patients most likely to not show up for their office appointment, BIDMC created a machine learning (ML)–based system that begins with (1) the appointment schedule depicted in the upper left. The schedule is fed into a ML platform hosted by Amazon Web Services (AWS), which generates no-show predictions (2). The ML platform in turn sends its intelligence to the short message service (SMS) platform, which sends out text messages to patients to remind them of their appointments (3). The SMS platform also uses an API to verify appointment status, sending that data to webOMR, the online EHR. The ML platform also sends a no-show score to the same EHR. Clinicians have access to a workflow tool to help manage all the data generated from the entire system. This tool is depicted in Figure 8.4B. (Courtesy of Beth Israel Deaconess Medical Center.)

Appointment Dashboard

Welcome **Si Wong** | Sign out

Patient

Appointment
4/29/2019 3:40 PM

HCA MEDICAL UNIT (SB)

KIM HANS S

Preferred Language Spanish

No Show Risk 0.00

Previous 5 appointments

Date/Time	Clinic	Provider	Kept?
2019-02-19 17:00:00	GYN CLINIC FPS (SR)	GOMEZ-CARRION,YVONNE	KEPT
2019-01-09 15:00:00	HCA MEDICAL UNIT (SB)	KIM HANS S	KEPT
2019-01-04 14:30:00	HCA MEDICAL UNIT (SB)	ROSE JONATHAN A	KEPT
2018-11-07 14:15:00	GYN CLINIC FPS (SR)	MESERVEY,MARYBETH A	KEPT
2018-11-05 15:30:00	HCA MEDICAL UNIT (SB)	GATOF EMILY S	KEPT

SMS Log

Date/Time Sent	Phone #	Message	Response
2019-02-28 10:50:00	(617) 123-4567	BIDMC: Your appt is @9:10am Wed 03/18/2019 in Healthcare Associates 617-754-9600	
2019-03-13 10:50:00	(617) 123-4567	BIDMC: Your appt is @9:10am Wed 03/18/2019 in Healthcare Associates 617-754-9600	NO

Activity Log

Date/Time	Intervention Method	Status	Notes	User
2019-04-25 09:52	PatientSite Email	Sent	This is a test	Si Wong
2019-04-25 09:52	Home Phone	Confirmed	Another test	Si Wong

New Activity Log Entry

Intervention Method   Home Phone   Follow Up Date   ☐ Intervention Complete

Status

Notes

Save

(B)

and deploy ML models. The goal of the new BIDMC system is to reach out to patients most likely to skip their appointments with electronic reminders—and to help clinicians manage their workflow more efficiently. The design of the ML system, which is illustrated in Figure 8.4, has generated measurable results. For the period ranging from Nov 11, 2018 to April 27, 2019, 355,499 office appointments were monitored in 245 clinics. Of these scheduled appointments, there were 35,942 no-shows (10.1%). The software platform predicted 54% of all the no-shows, with medium/high to high confidence (area under the curve 0.79).

Embracing Mobile Tools That Improve Clinical Decision Making

Truly informed decisions require that doctors and nurses have full access to as much patient data as possible. With that in mind, several healthcare organizations are tapping remote mobile-sensing devices that can provide details about patients' health status between office visits. BIDMC is taking the lead in this area as well, with the help of BIDMC@Home, a mobile app that connects patients to its customized EHR, webOMR. For patients willing to take their blood pressure at home on a regular basis, for instance, the app will send those readings to their physician for evaluation. BIDMC@Home takes advantage of Apple's CareKit, which the medical center has used to create a patient-facing program to give them more individualized instructions and advice. The BIDMCX CareKit app is described in more detail by Seth Berkowitz, MD, Director of Informatics Innovation and a staff radiologist at BIDMC:

> BIDMC@Home provides personalized home monitoring in many different conditions. HealthKit allows the app to collect data from various sensors and 3rd party apps to gain a holistic picture of health and help prevent hospital readmissions. Together with HealthKit-enabled wireless devices such as scales and blood pressure cuffs, patients with congestive heart failure can use BIDMC@Home to monitor vital signs and symptoms. Daily fluid, sodium intake and important predictors of fluid retention can also be imported via HealthKit. Connected thermometers allow patients with autoimmune diseases such as lupus and rheumatoid arthritis to better predict infections and monitor inflammation. Outpatient chemotherapy is associated with varied symptoms and side effects. The app allows these patients to better monitor their health during treatment.[2]

Because BIDMC@Home only gathers and displays information from the US Food and Drug Administration (FDA)–approved devices, it does not fall into the category that the federal agency calls software as a medical device (SaMD). Several other mobile apps, however, have required FDA clearance because they are considered medical devices. The agency recently published its guidelines on SaMD, which will help healthcare providers and developers navigate this evolving field and avoid unnecessary delays in launching new services. The FDA continues to classify software that is used for the diagnosis, treatment, cure, mitigation, or prevention of a disease or condition as a medical device, which requires various forms of FDA clearance, depending on the degree of risk it poses for patients.

The National Law Review's summary of the new FDA guidelines explains: "FDA clarified that software functions that are intended for maintaining or encouraging a healthy lifestyle and are unrelated to the diagnosis, cure, mitigation, prevention or treatment of a disease or condition are excluded from the definition of 'device.'"[3] On the other hand, if software or a mobile app is intended for diagnosis, cure, treatment, or prevention of a disease, it will be considered a medical device subject to the agency's clearance process if it falls into 3 specific categories[4]:

- Mobile apps that transform a mobile platform into a regulated medical device and therefore are the focus of the FDA's regulatory oversight: These mobile apps use a mobile platform's built-in features such as light, vibrations, camera, or other similar sources to perform medical device functions (e.g., mobile medical apps that are used by a licensed practitioner to diagnose or treat a disease).
- Software or mobile apps that connect to an existing device type for purposes of controlling its operation, function, or energy source, and therefore are the focus of the FDA's regulatory oversight.
- Software or mobile apps that are used in active patient monitoring to analyze patient-specific medical device data and therefore are mobile medical apps.

Examples of software or apps that fall into these 3 groups are explored in more detail in the inset text below.

FDA-Regulated Software as a Medical Device

The following list, provided by the US Food and Drug Administration (FDA), contains examples of device software functions that the agency regulates.[5] This list provides examples of software functions that are considered medical devices and on which the FDA will focus its regulatory oversight. These types of software meet the definition of device in the Federal Food, Drug, and Cosmetic Act, and their functionality poses a risk to a patient's safety if the software were to not function as intended. Each example below provides a list of possible relevant product code(s) and/or regulation number. The term "software functions" includes mobile applications (apps).

The FDA also encourages software manufacturers to search the FDA's public databases, such as the Product Classification database and the 510(k) Premarket Notification database, to determine the level of regulation for a given device and for the most up-to-date information about the relevant regulatory requirements.

Please also visit the device software function example page for a list of examples of FDA-approved or FDA-cleared software. The list is available at https://www.fda.gov/medical-devices/device-software-functions-including-mobile-medical-applications/examples-premarket-submissions-include-mmas-cleared-or-approved-fda.

Mobile apps that transform a mobile platform into a regulated medical device and, therefore, are the focus of the FDA's regulatory oversight: These mobile apps use a mobile platform's built-in features such as light, vibrations, camera, or other similar sources to perform medical-device functions (e.g., mobile medical apps that are used by a licensed practitioner to diagnose or treat a disease). Possible product codes: Varies depending on the intended use and function of the mobile medical app; see additional examples below of mobile medical apps that:

- Use a sensor or lead that is connected to a mobile platform to measure and display the electrical signal produced by the heart (electrocardiograph or ECG). Possible product code(s): DPS, MLC, OEY (21 CFR 870.2340), MLO, MWJ (21 CFR 870.2800).
- Use a sensor or electrode attached to the mobile platform or tools within the mobile platform itself (e.g., microphone and speaker) to electronically amplify and "project sounds associated with the heart, arteries and veins and other internal organs" (i.e., an electronic stethoscope). Possible product code: DQD (21 CFR 870.1875(b)).
- Use a sensor or electrode attached to the mobile platform or tools within the mobile platform itself (e.g., accelerometer) to measure physiological parameters during cardiopulmonary resuscitation (CPR) and give feedback about the quality of CPR being delivered. Possible product code: LIX (21 CFR 870.5200).
- Use a sensor attached to the mobile platform or tools within the mobile platform itself to record, view, or analyze eye movements for use in the diagnosis of balance disorders (i.e., nystagmograph). Possible product code: GWN (21 CFR 882.1460).

- Use tools within the mobile platform (e.g., speaker) to produce controlled levels of test tones and signals intended for use in conducting diagnostic hearing evaluations and assisting in the diagnosis of possible otologic disorders (i.e., an audiometer). Possible product code: EWO (21 CFR 874.1050).
- Use a sensor attached to the mobile platform or tools within the mobile platform itself (e.g., accelerometer) to measure the degree of tremor caused by certain diseases (i.e., a tremor transducer). Possible product code: GYD (21 CFR 882.1950).
- Use a sensor attached to the mobile platform or tools within the mobile platform itself (e.g., accelerometer, microphone) to measure physiological parameters (e.g., limb movement, electrical activity of the brain [EEG]) during sleep and are intended for use in diagnosis of specific diseases or conditions such as sleep apnea. Possible product code(s): OLV (21 CFR 882.1400), LEL, MNR (21 CFR 868.2375), FLS, NPF (21 CFR 868.2377).
- Use an attachment to the mobile platform to measure blood oxygen saturation for diagnosis of specific disease or condition. Possible product code(s): DQA, NLF, MUD, NMD (21 CFR 870.2700) or DPZ (21 CFR 870.2710).
- Present donor history questions to a potential blood donor and record and/or transmit the responses to those questions for a blood-collection facility to use in determining blood-donor eligibility prior to collection of blood or blood components. Possible product code: MMH (21 CFR 864.9165).
- Use an attachment to the mobile platform to measure blood glucose levels. Possible product code: NBW (21 CFR 862.1345).
- Use an attachment to the mobile platform (e.g., light source, laser) to treat acne, reduce wrinkles, or remove hair. Possible product code: OLP, OHT, OHS (21 CFR 878.4810), OZC (21 CFR 890.5740).
- Use a microphone or speaker within a mobile platform to serve as an audiometer to allow healthcare providers to determine hearing loss at different frequencies. Possible product code: EWO (21 CFR 874.1050).
- Analyze an image of a skin lesion using mathematical algorithms, such as fractal analysis, and provide the user with an assessment of the risk of the lesion.

Software functions that connect to an existing device type for purposes of controlling its operation, function, or energy source, and, therefore, are the focus of the FDA's regulatory oversight: These software functions are those that control the operation or function (e.g., changes settings) of an implantable or body-worn medical device.

Possible product codes: Varies depending on the intended use and function of the parent medical device; see additional examples below of software functions that:

- Alter the function or settings of an infusion pump. Possible product codes: MEB, FRN, LZH, LZG, OPP, MEA (21 CFR 880.5725), FIH (21 CFR 876.5820), LKK.
- Act as wireless remote controls or synchronization devices for computed tomography (CT) or X-ray machines. Possible product code: JAK (21 CFR 892.1750), IZL (21 CFR 892.1720), KPR (21 CFR 892.1680).
- Control or change settings of an implantable neuromuscular stimulator. Possible product code(s): GZC (21 CFR 882.5860).
- Calibrate, control, or change settings of a cochlear implant. Possible product code(s): MCM.
- Control the inflation or deflation of a blood-pressure cuff. Possible product code: DSJ (21 CFR 870.1100), DSK (21 CFR 870.1110), DXN (21 CFR 870.1130).
- Are used to calibrate hearing aids and assess the electroacoustic frequency and sound intensity characteristics emanating from a hearing aid, master hearing aid, group hearing aid, or group auditory trainer. Possible product code ETW (21 CFR 874.3310).

Software functions that are used in active patient monitoring to analyze patient-specific medical device data and, therefore, are the focus of the FDA's regulatory oversight, including software functions that:

- Acquire or process physiological signals that connect to bedside (or cardiac) monitors for active patient monitoring. Possible product code(s): DSI, MHX, MLD (21 CFR 870.1025), DRT, MWI, MSX (21 CFR 870.2300).
- Connect to a perinatal monitoring system and process uterine contraction and fetal heart rate data to another display to allow for remote monitoring of labor progress. Possible product code(s): HGM (21 CFR 884.2740).
- Are intended to process images for diagnostic review may be regulated as a picture-archiving and communications system. Possible product code LLZ, (21 CFR 892.2050).

If a software package or mobile app falls into one of these 3 categories, the agency may require developers to submit an application using one of three pathways:

- Premarket clearance, also called 510(k)
- Premarket approval
- De novo classification

In an effort to encourage digital innovation without fostering unreasonable risk to the public, the FDA has also stated that it will exercise "enforcement discretion" with regard to certain types of software, which is another way of saying the agency plans to take a hands-off position. The FDA states that products in this category may meet the definition of a medical device: "These software functions may be intended for use in the diagnosis of disease or other conditions, or in the cure, mitigation, treatment, or prevention of disease. Even though this software MAY meet the definition of medical device, FDA intends to exercise enforcement discretion for these types of software functions because they pose lower risk to the public."[5] The agency lists several examples of software that fall into this group. See the inset text below for examples.

Finally, the FDA provides examples of software that it says are clearly *not* medical devices and, therefore, not subject to its SaMD regulations. A partial list includes:

- Software functions that are intended to provide access to electronic "copies" (e.g., e-books, audio books) of medical textbooks or other reference materials with generic text-search capabilities
- Software functions that are intended for healthcare providers to use as educational tools for medical training or to reinforce training previously received
- Software functions that are intended for general patient education and facilitate patient access to commonly used reference information
- Software functions that automate general office operations in a healthcare setting
- Software functions that are generic aids or general-purpose products
- Software functions that are intended for individuals to log, record, track, evaluate, or make decisions or behavioral suggestions related to developing or maintaining general fitness, health, or wellness
- Software functions that provide patients with simple tools to organize and record their health information
- Software functions that are specifically marketed to help patients document, show, or communicate to providers regarding potential medical conditions

Examples of Software Functions for Which the FDA Intends to Exercise Enforcement Discretion[5]

1. Software functions that help patients with diagnosed psychiatric conditions (e.g., post-traumatic stress disorder (PTSD), depression, anxiety, obsessive compulsive disorder) maintain their behavioral coping skills by providing a "Skill of the Day" behavioral technique or audio messages that the user can access when experiencing increased anxiety;
2. Software functions that provide periodic educational information, reminders, or motivational guidance to smokers trying to quit, patients recovering from addiction, or pregnant women;
3. Mobile apps that use GPS location information to alert asthmatics of environmental conditions that may cause asthma symptoms or alert an addiction patient (substance abusers) when near a pre-identified, high-risk location;
4. Software functions that use video and video games to motivate patients to do their physical therapy exercises at home;
5. Software functions that prompt a user to enter which herb and drug they would like to take concurrently and provide information about whether interactions have been seen in the literature and a summary of what type of interaction was reported;
6. Software functions that use patient characteristics such as age, sex, and behavioral risk factors to provide patient-specific screening, counseling, and preventive recommendations from well-known and established authorities;
7. Software functions that use a checklist of common signs and symptoms to provide a list of possible medical conditions and advice on when to consult a healthcare provider;
8. Software functions that guide a user through a questionnaire of signs and symptoms to provide a recommendation for the type of healthcare facility most appropriate to their needs;
9. Software functions that are intended to allow a user to initiate a pre-specified nurse call or emergency call using broadband or cellular phone technology;
10. Software functions that enable a patient or caregiver to create and send an alert or general emergency notification to first responders;
11. Software functions that keep track of medications and provide user-configured reminders for improved medication adherence;
12. Software functions that provide patients a portal into their own health information, such as access to information captured during a previous clinical visit or historical trending and comparison of

vital signs (e.g., body temperature, heart rate, blood pressure, or respiratory rate);

13. Software functions that aggregate and display trends in personal health incidents (e.g., hospitalization rates or alert notification rates);

14. Software functions that allow a user to collect (electronically or manually entered) blood pressure data and share this data through e-mail, track and trend it, or upload it to a personal or electronic health record;

15. Software functions that provide oral health reminders or tracking tools for users with gum disease;

16. Software functions that provide prediabetes patients with guidance or tools to help them develop better eating habits or increase physical activity;

17. Software functions that display, at opportune times, images or other messages for a substance abuser who wants to stop addictive behavior;

18. Software functions that provide drug–drug interactions and relevant safety information (side effects, drug interactions, active ingredient) as a report based on demographic data (age, gender), clinical information (current diagnosis), and current medications.

Technological Approach to Diagnostic Error Detection

One of the recurring themes in this book has been the need to address the numerous diagnostic errors that continue to plague clinicians. In Chapter 1, we pointed out that about 12 million adult outpatients a year are affected by some sort of diagnostic error, which translates into 1 out of 20 Americans.[6] Although the solution to this epidemic requires a multifactorial approach, technology can play a major role. Avera Creighton Hospital has joined forces with the University of California San Francisco (UCSF), using an artful blend of human and artificial intelligence to address the diagnostic error problem.[7]

The hospital realized it needed to develop a more organized way to identify these problems, and along with UCSF, created a "process that ensures a timely root cause analysis for cases involving diagnostic error."[7] The process involved a review of 7-day hospital admissions, autopsy findings, mortality statistics, and patient self-reports. This analysis, combined with the Safer DX instrument and a fishbone diagram, has proven useful in getting at the root causes of many diagnostic mishaps. The analysis, which ran for 3 months in 2018, looked at almost 2,000 discharges and 85 7-day readmissions. A review of 77 of these readmissions revealed 9 diagnostic errors (12%). These errors involved chol-angitis, liver abscess, cancer-related GI bleeding, a lupus flare-up, and periton-sillar abscess. The review process gave clinicians and administrators a better sense of what their deficiencies were: "The most common categories of root cause included laboratory/radiology tests and assessment. The most common subcategories were failure or delay in ordering needed test(s), erroneous clini-cian interpretation of test, and failure or delay to recognize or weigh urgency." Equally important, the program gave the hospital and medical center a way to create a network of clinicians and staffers who wanted feedback on diagnostic error cases. Traditionally, physicians have always been reluctant to report their own mistakes or those of their co-workers.

Aymer Al-Mutairi, MD, with the Department of Family and Community Medicine at Baylor College of Medicine, Houston, Texas, and his colleagues developed and tested the aforementioned Safer Dx Instrument on 389 patient records with the goal of creating a tool that could help clinicians spot patients at high risk of experiencing a diagnostic error before it occurs.[8] The instrument they constructed consisted of 12 questions, asking practitioners to rate each episode of care under review on a scale of 1 to 6, strongly agree to strongly dis-agree. Issues investigated included whether the patient encounter suggested an alternative diagnosis that was not considered, whether the physical exam or test-ing data suggested an alternative, whether there were red flag signs or symptoms that should have been taken into account, and whether the diagnostic workup should have prompted additional diagnostic evaluation with tests or consults.

The retrospective analysis was performed at a Veterans Affairs site using trigger algorithms to identify patients with possible diagnostic errors based on unexpected hospitalizations and return visits. The Safer Dx tool generated an overall accuracy of 84%, sensitivity of 71%, specificity of 90%, negative predic-tive value of 86%, and positive predictive value of 78%, when compared to an analysis of an earlier patient-record sample.

Kaiser Permanente is another organization that is taking advantage of new digital tools to help reduce the risk of diagnostic errors. It has created a SureNet program that is powered by the organization's EHR system to detect patients who might easily fall through the cracks and develop serious complications down the road. It has developed over 50 projects to ensure more accurate diag-noses early in a patient's course. For example, when a patient presents with gross hematuria, their urine specimens are followed up by a urologist for a more thorough workup. In a 1-year period, this gross hematuria screening initiative resulted in 980 patients referred to a specialist and 3 cases of cancer detected.[7] Similarly, an abdominal aortic aneurysm (AAA) screening program makes sure that patients with an AAA get proper follow-up. "In four years, KP SureNet has ordered 2,625 ultrasounds and sent 1,464 vascular surgery referrals. Following intervention from the program, 185 patients have had surgical intervention for abdominal aortic aneurysms."

Similarly, Kaiser Permanente Southern California has a SureNet program to capture patients who are at risk for end-stage renal disease (ESRD) by making sure that any patient whose initial creatinine level is abnormal has a follow-up creatinine test performed. John Sim, MD, and his colleagues identified more than 12,000 patients who had abnormal creatinine levels, identified through EHRs. This cohort had an estimated glomerular filtration rate below 60 ml/min and had not undergone a repeat lab analysis for at least 90 days. A centralized regional nurse coordinated with clinicians to contact patients about the need for a second test. Among the 12,394 patients with initial elevated creatinine readings, approximately 87% had eGFR readings between 45 and 59 ml/min. Among nearly 7,000 patients who had a second creatinine test, more than half (53.3%) were found to have chronic kidney disease. Over time, 83 of these patients developed end-stage disease, demonstrating that the SureNet program had a positive impact on patient care.[9]

Promising Solutions, Unrealistic Expectations

In these 8 chapters, we have outlined many of the most promising tools that are addressing the diagnostic-errors dilemma. We began this analysis with a discussion of the metrics being used to measure the extent of the problem, including postmortem reviews, medical records, malpractice claims data, health insurance claims, physician surveys, and patient surveys. The evidence indicates that all these yardsticks have their shortcomings. As Chapter 1 pointed out, there are new approaches, including the Symptom-Disease Pair Analysis of Diagnostic Error or SPADE system, which may improve the way we track diagnostic errors.

We also discussed a long list of contributing causes for diagnostic errors, including poorly designed EHRs, inadequate communication among clinicians and between clinicians and patients, disruptive physical environments in which diagnostic decisions must be made, and cognitive errors. The latter issue allowed us to dive into Type 1 and Type 2 reasoning, along with their strengths and weaknesses.

In Chapter 2, we highlighted the promise of AI- and ML-fueled solutions, including neural networks and random forest modeling. These tools are now impacting gastroenterology, ophthalmology, oncology, cardiology, endocrinology, critical care medicine, medication management, and a host of other specialties. And although these advances are already affecting the day-to-day care of patients, critical thinking and caution are still required to evaluate these emerging tools. Some rely solely on a retrospective analysis of patient data, have not been tested on several different patient populations, or have used data sets that are not "clean" enough to justify their use.

With these concerns in mind, it was necessary to devote an entire chapter to AI criticisms, obstacles, and limitations. Physician surveys indicate that many remain skeptical about the value of AI and ML in patient care. One of the most contentious issues that confront technologists and clinicians alike is the black box phenomenon. The data science, advanced statistics, and mind-bending mathematical equations supporting many ML algorithms turn many physicians away. We took a closer look at this issue in Chapter 3, but an editorial in the *Journal of Family Practice* provides an effective argument for those who do not want to use software when the mechanism of action is too difficult to comprehend. Referring to AI tools to screen for diabetic retinopathy and colon cancer, John Hickner, MD, MSc, the Editor in Chief, states: "These tools were developed with very sophisticated computer programs, but they are not unlike a plethora of clinical decision aids already widely used in primary care for diagnosis and risk assessment, such as the Ottawa Ankle Rules, the Gail Model for breast cancer risk, the FRAX tool for osteoporosis-related fracture risk, the ASCVD Risk Calculator for cardiovascular risk, and the CHA2DS2-VASC score for prediction of thrombosis and bleeding risk from anticoagulation therapy."[10]

One of the most promising yet least publicized aspects of ML is its potential role in data analytics. The research summarized in Chapter 5 demonstrates that in order to reinvent CDS, it is necessary to reinvent how subgroup analysis is performed by employing the state-of-the-art ML tools, including random forest modeling, proportional hazards regression, logistic regression, and penalized logistic regression.

We have also described several vendors that continue to update their clinical decision support systems to keep pace with developments in AI and ML, Although these sophisticated CDS systems are helping many thousands of practitioners improve diagnosis and treatment, some enthusiastic users still have unrealistic expectations about their impact on diagnostic errors—for at least 2 reasons. As we point out several times, the list of contributing factors that lead to diagnostic mishaps is long, and many of these problems require better communication not more technology. Secondly, currently available CDS systems have yet to fully incorporate the findings of systems biology and precision medicine, the topics of Chapters 6 and 7.

Despite these shortcomings, we nonetheless come back to the same conclusion stated in our preface: AI will never replace a competent physician. That said, there's little doubt that a competent physician who uses all the tools that AI has to offer will soon replace the competent physician who ignores these tools.

References

1. Amazon Comprehend Medical. "Extract Information from Unstructured Medical Text Accurately and Quickly." Accessed November 1, 2019, Retrieved from https://aws.amazon.com/comprehend/medical/
2. Berkowitz, S. (2016, November 23). "The BIDMC CareKit App." *Life as a Healthcare CIO.* Retrieved from http://geekdoctor.blogspot.com/2016/11/the-bidmc-carekit-app.html
3. Pollard, V. T., Ryan, M. W., Mohanty, A., and Kaur, G. (2019, October 3). "Is Your Software a Medical Device? FDA Issues Six Digital Health Guidance Documents." *National Law Review.* Retrieved from https://www.natlawreview.com/article/your-software-medical-device-fda-issues-six-digital-health-guidance-documents
4. US Food and Drug Administration. (2019, September 26). "Examples of Device Software Functions the FDA Regulates." Retrieved from https://www.fda.gov/medical-devices/device-software-functions-including-mobile-medical-applications/examples-device-software-functions-fda-regulates
5. Food and Drug Administration. (2019, September 27). "Policy for Device Software Functions and Mobile Medical Applications Guidance for Industry and Food and Drug Administration Staff." Retrieved from https://www.fda.gov/media/80958/download
6. National Academies of Sciences, Engineering, and Medicine. (2015). *Improving Diagnosis in Health Care.* Washington (DC): National Academies Press.
7. Health Research & Educational Trust. (2018, September). *Improving Diagnosis in Medicine Change Package.* Chicago (IL): Health Research & Educational Trust. Retrieved from http://www.hret-hiin.org/
8. Al-Mutairi, A., Meyer, A. N., Thomas, E. J., Etchegaray, J. M., Roy, K. M., Davalos, M. C., Sheikh, S., and Singh, H. (2016). "Accuracy of the Safer Dx Instrument to Identify Diagnostic Errors in Primary Care." *Journal of General Internal Medicine,* vol. 31, pp. 602–608.
9. Sim, J. J., Batech, M., Danforth, K. N., Rutkowski, M. P., Jacobsen, S. J., and Kanter, M. H. (2017). "End-Stage Renal Disease Outcomes among the Kaiser Permanente Southern California Creatinine Safety Program (Creatinine SureNet): Opportunities to Reflect and Improve." *Permanente Journal,* vol. 21, pp. 16–143.
10. Hickner J. (2019). "It's Time to Get to Know AI." *Journal of Family Practice,* vol. 68, p. 479. Retrieved from https://www.mdedge.com/familymedicine/article/211891/oncology/its-time-get-know-ai

Index

Systematic Blood Pressure
   Intervention Trial (SPRINT), 97,
   108
systematic literature surveillance, 78
Systematized Nomenclature of
   Medicine (SNOMED), 71
systems biology, 42, 105–111, 114,
   115, 118–120, 156

T

TACo. *See* targeted automatic
   e-consultation
targeted automatic e-consultation
   (TACo), 133
Tesseract OCR, 141
TNF-α. *See* tumor necrosis factor-α
Topol, Eric, 65
transcriptomics, 115, 118, 119
tumor necrosis factor-α (TNF-α),
   125–127
Type 1 thinking, 7, 10
Type 2 thinking, 7, 10
Tyrer-Cuzick (TC) model, 32

U

University of Copenhagen Center for
   Advanced Studies in Biomedical
   Innovation Law, 65

UpToDate, 78, 83, 84, 125
US Preventive Services Task Force,
   98

V

variants of uncertain clinical
   significance (VUS), 101, 102
Viscensia, 116
VisualDX, 80, 81, 83
vital signs index (VSI), 116
VSI. *See* vital signs index
VUS. *See* variants of uncertain
   clinical significance

W

Wainberg, Michael, 61, 63
Wang, Pu, 34, 35
webOMR, 141, 144, 146
Wolters Kluwer, 25, 78, 83, 84

Y

Yala, Adam, 32

Z

Zech, John, 64
Zio EKG monitor, 36